Gathering Wisdom

Gathering Wisdom

How To
Acquire Wisdom
From Others
While Developing
Your Own

Jerry Fletcher
Cheryl Matschek, M.S., M.H.
Al Siebert, PH.D.
Gail Tycer, M.S.

Practical Psychology Press
Portland, Oregon

Practical Psychology Press
P.O. Box 535
Portland, OR 97207

Book Design: Z-axis Marketing, Inc.
Cover Design: Z-axis Marketing, Inc.

Printed in the United States of America

Library of Congress Cataloging-in-Publication Data

Gathering wisdom: How to acquire wisdom from others while developing your own/Jerry Fletcher ... [et al.].
    p.   cm.
  Includes index.
  ISBN 0-944227-28-7
  1. Success--Psychological aspects. 2. Success in business,
  I. Fletcher, Jerry L.

BF637.S8 G37 2002
158 -- dc21
                                                    2002034885

Dedication

For
Seekers,
the
ones who
know
they must find out
on their own
but
are not afraid
to question,
to listen,
and to
gather wisdom
from the
experience
of
others.

Contents

The
Flame
of
Wisdom

Quorum Members

What is Wisdom?

Wisdom can be gathered.
Wisdom can be learned, or gained.
Wisdom cannot be taught.

That much we agree on. As the four of us talked about writing this book, we realized that our best service to you would be to serve as your coaches; to share with you the things we have learned along the way. And then, fully confident of your ability to learn, to allow you to apply to your own life what we have to say.

What is wisdom? We talked about what wisdom means to each of us in many meetings during several years.

We asked ourselves, "If I could go back and talk to the person I was when I started my career, what would I say?"

Cheryl says:
We often use words we think we understand, until someone asks us to define them. Then we are faced with the startling realization that we're—well, not quite sure; not definite; well, it's kind of like this; or Gosh, I think I need a dictionary. Even then, sometimes, the dictionary just doesn't quite fill the bill. We read the definition and find that something is still missing. And that's the way with wisdom.

Wisdom. We all have heard of it. We all have used it. But few of us, if any, can offer a definition that everyone would totally agree with...or that everyone would agree is all-encompassing.

In that light, I offer to you what "wisdom" means to me. I might add, too, that my definition comes not from Webster, but instead from my understanding of the Holy Bible. For to me that is where all wisdom begins: *it is from our God, our creator. It is not merely the result of human ability or effort* (Proverbs 2:6).

Wisdom provides guidance in the way of righteousness (Proverbs 4:10-19). It is very precious...it reveals itself with grace, preserves character, requires trust, teachability, servanthood, responsiveness, and reliance on God. It is the exact opposite of autonomy and arrogance. James 3:13-17 goes further, saying that it is *peace-loving, considerate, submissive, full of mercy and good fruits, impartial and sincere.* This suggests to me that wisdom doesn't take sides, does no harm, and requires understanding of others. It has a distinct element of humility that comes from and with it, as well as prudence and discretion. It is clear that inherent in wisdom, then, is the use of sound judgment further establishing that wisdom is just.

Applying wisdom to our human, earthly lives, I would say that wisdom is the ability to use the best means at the best time to accomplish the best ends. It is not merely a matter of information or knowledge but of skillful and practical application of the truth to the ordinary events of life. It is awareness to be sensitive to this situation, to this person, uninfluenced by any corruption of the past. I would even go a step further and say that wisdom relates to developing an eternal perspective on life.

I would venture that few today know wisdom's value. The fear of the Lord is wisdom, showing respect and reverence for God and shunning evil. I reiterate, to me it is the only way to attain true wisdom. To fear God is to nurture an attitude of awe and humility before Him and to walk in total dependence upon God in every area of life. That is wisdom.

Al says,
What is wisdom? How does anyone become wise? Is it something you are, something you have, or something you do? Does anyone ever set out to develop or acquire wisdom as a goal? How does a person become wise? Do people regarded as wise think of themselves as wise? What is it about someone that has others see them as wise?

Dr. Judith Ramaley enjoyed working in university administration at the University of Nebraska. She knew that one day she would become a university president. In 1982, Ramaley became the chief academic officer at the State University of New York at Albany and was acting president.

Judith developed a plan for learning about how to be a highly effective university president. At conferences for administrators in higher education, she would single out university presidents and interview them about what their experience had taught them about how to be effective. She asked what they wished they had known when they first started. She asked what to do quickly and what mistakes to avoid. She was told, for example, that some professors would be among the first people who would want to see her and they would present a long list of charges maligning an administrator that they had conflicts with. The professors who try to get to her first with their complaints, she was told, will prove in the years ahead to be the ones most likely to stir up faculty and staff antagonism toward her.

Judith took notes and created a small manual for herself about how to succeed as a university president. When she was hired to become president of Portland State University in 1990 she was ready. The wisdom she had collected from dozens of interviews significantly shortened her learning curve. She took hold of the position with self-confidence. She did many things right with the faculty, students, administrators, alumni, and the local community.

In the seven years that she was at Portland State, she instigated long-needed reforms, reworked the curriculum, downsized the staff, and created an impressive record. In 1997 she left Portland State to become President of the University of Vermont.

Wise people have accurate, perceptive insights into human behavior and understand how things work. They are observers of human nature, are master psychologists with excellent emotional intelligence. They have learned what they know from real life experience, not from academic study. They generally keep what they know to themselves, but are willing to share what they know with certain individuals. They are available to give advice to open-minded learners. They have a talent for asking questions that lead to new understanding. Are conscious of themselves, and can communicate what they know when they choose to.

Wise people are smart about what they do and don't do. They have an inner frame of reference for their actions and statements. They "read" situations well and understand others accurately. Can see through the obvious. Trust their intuition. Have a sense of hidden motives behind the actions of others. Are less vulnerable to cons, threats, criticism, and manipulators. Handle pressure and threats with humor. Remain stable and sustain equanimity in times of turmoil. Want and expect things to work well. They feel optimistic and self-confident when coping with rough situations.

A valuable way to understand something is to define what it is not. What is the opposite of wisdom? It is to:
- speak or act in stupid ways, then blame others for what happens.
- speak or act in ways that cause difficulties for people or groups important to you.
- speak or act in ways that lead to unnecessary loss.
- not learn from mistakes, make the same mistakes.
- be out of touch with what is happening.
- be bitter about the past, cynical about the future.
- be outspoken about what others are doing wrong.
- act in ways contrary to one's stated values and goals, and not know it.

How does a person acquire wisdom? It develops from life-long, child-like curiosity and a playful spirit. Wise people are happy rather than hostile, no matter how badly life has treated them. You gain wisdom when you ask questions, explore, want to know how thing work, and learn valuable lessons from rough experiences.

Gail says:
A friend of mine defines wisdom as a three-part process: (1) information; (2) knowledge; and, finally, (3) wisdom. Information, of course, is the raw data — the kind of stuff you can find in books, in the research, on the internet. Knowledge is knowing how to apply the information. And wisdom is knowing when, and under what circumstances, the information and the knowledge are appropriate, or useful, or even true. And when

and how — and even whether — to apply the knowledge you
have gained.

Another friend thinks of wisdom this way: "Wisdom is bring-
ing all of your knowledge and skill to a situation to bring it to
a successful conclusion."

If there's ever a lull in the conversation, try asking the group,
"What is wisdom?" I guarantee a lively conversation!

I believe that personal wisdom begins with knowing who —
and whose — we are. And in living by a values system consistent with that understanding. In seeing, and in appreciating,
the unique gifts we have been given as personality traits and
capabilities; as opportunities, and as outright things! Appreciation, too, is part of wisdom.

When I think of wisdom, I think of a client I worked with
many years ago. A truly wise man, even though his formal
education had gone only as far as the third grade. A fair and
honest man of integrity and great wisdom. A man who understood, and consistently lived by his values. And a man who,
along the way, managed to build a multi-billion dollar empire.

As part of my assignment to write a company video for this
man, I had the unique privilege of "shadowing" him for several days — sitting in on all his business meetings; listening as
he made his decisions. What a wonderful way to get inside
that remarkable thought process! I found a man with a clear,
and sometimes rather stubborn, vision; unshakable in his
determination to act in what he saw as the "right" way. And
that's how he built his empire: by looking first at how he
could benefit others, and then by taking the steps to derive
mutual benefit from each decision he made.

He stuck by his same suppliers, even when someone else might charge less in the short term, reckoning that if he did right by them, they would do right by him. He was seldom disappointed. He believed strongly in the future, and in his part in it. He planned for good times — and bad, so he had nothing to fear. And he refused to accept that anything could not be done. When conventional ways did not work, he found another way to get what was needed.

Of the many inspiring lessons I learned from him during that time, one stands out very clearly. It happened that some months before, one of his most trusted executives had made what turned out to be a devastatingly poor decision, ultimately costing the company millions. And yet, the executive remained in place.

Strongly pressed at a Board meeting to fire that executive, he refused, because "I paid enough tuition for him to learn that lesson; I don't want him going to school on me, and using what he's learned for the competition."

That's wisdom.

Jerry says:

Wisdom is knowing your limits and your resources.

Being all wise is not for me.

I know that I can't know everything, yet I'm certain that I know someone who knows someone who knows the answers I'm seeking.

By stringing together connections to as many of the people who will share those pearls of wisdom as I possibly can, I tap into a treasure trove of truth, beauty, and pragmatic advice that has stood the test of time.

Sometimes that takes a little faith — like Tyler, the company president who had given up only to find that sometimes the shortest distance between you and your objective is a circle.

Or the confidence to go "pearl diving," to "work the room" for fun, profit,and possibly for love.

Sometimes it is cold hard facts — the kind that keep a politico in power and can provide the practical advice you need about technologies that are wise in the ways of managing contacts.

Occasionally it is a piece of advice from a much-traveled friend, like Bob, my buddy with the razor-sharp mind in a rumpled suit.

Or like Sam Gamgee, one of the characters in Tolkien's The Lord of the Rings trilogy.

Early on in the story, stolid Sam agrees to accompany Frodo Baggins on the journey that will decide the fate of their world. Along the way, Sam recalls bits of advice from the "Gaffer" (his Grandfather) and stoically carries them out for at least two further books into the story.

The Gaffer's wisdom pays off. Without it, the "one ring to find them, one ring to bind them" would have wound up in the wrong hands.

Plain, plodding Sam knows his limits and trusts his "Gaffer."

Ultimately, whether you are building a business, a career, or a life of joy, it is neither what you know nor whom you know that matters so much as whom you trust — and who trusts you.

Those trusting relationships with customers and contractors, managers and mentors, friends and family, form your personal network. Networking through them, simply asking for their help, gives you access to the wisdom of the ages.

It begins with one contact at a time — one gem of a contact plus another and yet another until you have a string of them — like a beautiful string of pearls.

And so, while we all may come from differing points of view, we are united in one goal: to save you time and pain; to help you as you make your life better. To help you see how the pieces fit. To share the practical insights each of us has acquired from the thousands of people who have come to our presentations and workshops; who have read our books, and counseled with us. To help you build a richer, fuller life of boundless success.

We start with the inner you and progress to focusing outward on others. Cheryl Matschek will share her thoughts on nurturing a vision, and on inspiring others to build it with you. Al Siebert will help you to build your resilience. Gail Tycer will help you develop techniques for communicating well with others. Jerry Fletcher will show you how to network effectively.

Let's get started!

Finding
The Flame
Within

Cheryl Matschek, M.S., M.H.

Values:
Foundation for Meaningful Success

Many people are outwardly successful, but inwardly are unhappy, unfulfilled, and needlessly stressed. They may have the dream home, the car they've always wanted, the right title, and an overflowing bank account or investment portfolio. And yet, they may not be happy.

Although this book is about success, and when we think about success it is usually business success, it wouldn't be complete without considering the personal and spiritual dimension of our lives. It is from these aspects of our being that meaning and purpose are derived. Life is not separated neatly into separate compartments — personal, professional, social, spiritual, etc. Nor can we separate the parts by applying differing values or principles to each. In other words, it is not possible to live one set of values at the office and another set of values when you are at home, out socially, or at church. Trying to live life in distinct compartments with differing values causes conflict, frustration, anxiety, and distress, and it puts relationships in great jeopardy.

What many are missing in their lives, no matter how much they have materially, is a sense of meaning. Many feel the unrest of accomplishment without meaning, of acquisition without satisfaction, or of running to the next stop without understanding the destination. Does this describe you? Are you on this treadmill as well? This is a spiritual question because it is about ultimate values and concerns. The need for meaning is not biological. It isn't even psychological. Rather, it is spiritual.

As you think about success in your life, it is really important to consider what success really means to you. And if you do take the time and energy to determine this, you'll first have to examine your character, ethics, morals, and ultimately, values. One caution here. You may be just entering the business world and feel this isn't an issue — yet. Unfortunately, by the time it becomes an issue it is much harder to change and turn around. The best time to ponder these questions and become clear in your mind and heart about your values, and your commitment to them, is now. When you do, you will have clear direction that will guide your morals and ethics, build character, and help you live a life of integrity.

It takes a whole life to build a character and one minute to tear it down. The real test of character, perhaps, is what you would do if you knew you'd never get caught, or knew that no one was watching. It is who you are when no one is watching — who you are at the heart level. Character is what you control about yourself. Francois de la Rouchefoucald said, *"Weakness of character is the only defect that cannot be amended."* Another puts it this way, "One judge of character is by a man and how he treats those who can do nothing for him."

Integrity is closely aligned with character. When you act with integrity you come from the wholeness of who you are. Integrity means walking our talk. It means carrying through on what you say you will do, and living out what you say is important to you. When we live a life of integrity we provide not only a more peaceful existence for ourselves, but a meaningful model for others to do the same.

Our society places so much importance on the material aspects of our existence. More, bigger, better, higher, faster, newer, quicker, greater—you name it. It's great to have a nice home and the comforts we have come to think of as necessities, but when do we say "enough"? We become so involved with the *having* and *getting*, and as a result the *doing*, that we miss the *being*. Ralph Waldo Emerson once said, *"Nothing gives so much direction to a person's life as a sound set of values."*

How about you? Have you asked yourself what you value personally? Do you really know what is important in your life? Do you place more importance on investments or money than relationships? If you say your marriage is important to you, are you making an investment of time and energy into it? Do you believe that being healthy is an important part of your life? And if you do, are you living in such a way that promotes health?

Let's ask, and answer, a few directed questions right now. Don't put it off. If you do, you might not get back to it. A few areas or qualities or characteristics to consider, or at least get you thinking about what you value, are these: God, family, marriage, trustworthiness, integrity, service, loyalty, honesty, courtesy, commitment, encouragement, ethics, compassion, attitude, sincerity, courage, respect, excellence, fidelity, spirituality, and health.

What is really important to me?

What do I really want in my life?

What do I want to become?

Where am I spiritually? Where do I want to be?

Am I clear about my values or am I actually living my life based on someone else's values?

What is the purpose of my marriage — of my family?

Am I headed in a direction that will take me to a place I want to be?

Am I taking the time to develop the important relationships in my life (spouse, children, family, friends) or am I too busy filling it up with work-related activities to increase income and not finding time to develop and maintain relationships?

How much time do I spend every day with my spouse, one-on-one, communicating and building our relationship?

How much time do I take with each child on a daily basis?

Do I make time for my friends — or am I so busy that I no longer take time to keep the relationship growing?

Am I making time to give back to my community?

How important is my health? And what am I doing to make sure that I remain as healthy as I can possibly be?

Do I have a healthy attitude towards finances?

Am I really clear how my business or career fits into my life — with balance?

What about ethics? What does this mean to me and what does ethical behavior mean?

Bottom line, what are the core values that are more important to you than anything else? And what attitude and behaviors mirror these values? And then — are you living your life according to what you just identified? Are you walking your talk?

As you ask yourself these questions, if you don't necessarily like the answers — or if you find you really can't even answer the question — it's time to look within and examine the contents. Values are the foundation of character. And we are responsible for our characters — not God, not mom or dad, not the church, the state, the government, our boss, or anyone else. "If we don't know what we stand for," the old saying goes, "we'll fall for anything." If we're not clear about what is truly important to us, we will find difficulty in the face of trying or tempting circumstances to confidently make a decision regarding behavior and actions.

What's the verdict? Are you living out what you say is important to you? Are your behaviors and values in alignment? Again, if they are not, the net result is conflict, distress, disharmony, anxiety, and a host of other negatives.

As we make this personal inventory, you might find that you have said certain things are important to you — but you have not been acting in ways consistent with those values. That's okay for now. In fact, most people, when they first examine their values and behavior, will find they are not the same. Many people realize for the first time that they've never taken the time to identify what is truly important to them. They may find they've been motivated by what others think, expect, or do, rather than being internally motivated by what is deeply believed. What is important is that we allow this to awaken us and help us move forward to begin

living out what we say is truly important in our lives, by
aligning our behavior with our values.

The story is legion about the business person (man or woman)
who amasses a great fortune but loses a marriage; or the person who has no relationship with a grown child because time
wasn't invested with the child when he or she was younger; or
the individual who has every "thing" they have ever dreamed
of, but is no longer healthy because no attention was given to
taking care of the needs of the body. Why do we do this to
ourselves and to our families?   Is it because we don't know
any better? Or is it because we haven't asked ourselves the
values questions and established our priorities. Either way, it
is important to recognize that every single minute we are alive
we are trading that moment of life for something in return.
Are you happy with the trade? Really happy with the trade?
And if you are just beginning on the career path — where do
you want to end up? Take this to heart: If you are not happy
now, you will not be any happier with "more" of anything!

The foundation of our lives needs to be secure, and that means
knowing what is truly important. For me it is God, second is
my family, and third is business. What about you — how clear
are you about your values? Or will it take an unexpected,
unwanted wake-up call to force you to take a look. When
we're not clear about our values, temptation creeps into our
lives through many doorways. And, it is the inability or un-
willingness to resist temptation that often gets us into trouble
or on some distant path leading us in a direction away from
our dreams, beliefs, and values. If we are to remain on track,
we must do four things:

- We must hold fast to what we say is important and not be weakened by situations. This means we must not give in to circumstances or situations that compromise our values, our integrity.

- We must not be deceived by the persuasive attempts of others to pull us off course and in a direction that goes against what we believe in.

- We must stand on commitment, not emotion. That means we must pull ourselves back to our principles and values and forego an emotional pull that may seem fun or really rewarding at the time, but leads us to an unhealthy, compromising situation.

- We must not be enamored with instant gratification. We must not confuse something that can give immediate results, pleasure, etc. that is *for the moment* and pulls us away from our values.

These are principles we must live by, in every area of our lives if we are to live with harmony, peace, fulfillment, joy and integrity. We will never feel truly successful or completely enjoy our vocations if we violate our personal values in the process. Much like a garden, we must keep our plot clean of weeds, and plant the strong, healthy principles that hold up our values. Living our life by principles isn't a fad, nor is it a program. It becomes the way we live — *it is everything we do.* Our values provide us an internal compass. When we live from our values we keep from burning out. When we do what we do, personally and professionally, consistent with our values, then we will love what we do. Once you are clear about this, you have your blueprint for everything else—vision, mission, systems, procedures, actions, behavior, attitudes, decisions—all of it. You can bring into alignment your walk and your talk. Align your strategic decisons and day-to-day actions with your guiding values.

As stated earlier, it is my belief that the problem we face is a spiritual one. It is not one of money, or having enough, or doing enough. It comes from the inside. It has to do with meaning, with being, with eternity. Only you can decide where you are, spiritually. But I can tell you this, and I believe it from the bottom of my heart: If you haven't yet determined clearly for yourself why we are here on this planet, and where we go when we leave here, then you haven't yet found the greatest, most important fact of life. And when that is missing, you'll never experience the joy or the satisfaction in your work or at home or anywhere else. And, I believe, if you haven't answered this question, it will really be difficult to establish clear values that make much sense.

It is having a changeless core of values on the inside that allows us the freedom and ability to change in these times of rapid transformation. When we learn that it isn't what is on the outside that brings us fulfillment, then we will have made a great discovery. Just as you won't change a poor marriage by paying attention to someone else, and you won't change the look of your kitchen by painting the bedroom, neither will we change the results we are getting in our lives by changing the outside. The change must take place on the inside first…where character, integrity, values, and ethics are born.

Businesses today yearn for leaders who stand for something more than just the bottom line. Your values should be the basis for all you do in business. Regardless of what changes occur in any industry, or in the personnel of a business, or in the challenges you face, values are what remain unchanged. The quality of your business life, indeed your entire life, will be a direct result of your values, and how resolutely you hold to them.

Leaders must have a strong belief system to deal with the challenges of today's world, and to maintain their convictions. They must be morally strong. The principles that come to mind are those of truth, honesty, and justice — and they are essential. Be clear about your values — hold fast to your principles, live a life of integrity, and you will indeed be successful far beyond your imagination, and in ways that are so much more important than the limited vision of success that too many fall for.

James Allen, well known author of *As A Man Thinketh*, wrote, "From the state of man's heart proceeds the condition of his life; his thoughts blossom into deeds, and his deeds bear the fruitage of character and destiny."

Principled Leadership

Seventy percent of Fortune 1000 organizations cite lack of trained leaders as their number one barrier to growth, according to a recent statistic. Nevertheless, many companies, from the smallest to the largest, do little or even nothing to develop leaders within their organizations, or to develop leadership succession (planning future leadership for the organization).

Leadership, whether you are *the* leader or *a* leader, is an important part of business success (or family success, for that matter). Regardless of the type of business you are in, leadership is an important element that determines whether or not the business will be mediocre, marginally successful, or highly successful. It very well might be the difference between the business making it, or going the way of bankruptcy, or simply closing doors.

Shortly after take-off for any air flight, when I am in the air thousands of feet above the ground, I look out the window and realize how different my perspective is from such a height. It is so much easier to see more of the "whole" from the air and to see how pieces fit together. It always reminds me of the larger perspective that is required of leaders.

Organizations are amidst tremendous change today, and that change isn't over. It seems with every year that passes the change comes faster and more furiously than ever before. This can be an exciting adventure, or we can go through it kicking and screaming, or perhaps take the opposite approach and keep our heads buried in the sand so we don't notice what is happening all around us. Unfortunately, there are many leaders who do just this. Leadership requires courage to let go of *what was* when it is time to move forward to more effective, efficient solutions. It has taken us years to discover that we live in a quantum world and now that we understand this, we need to change what we do. All of us, but especially leaders, must move with flexibility; rather than describe tasks alone, we must facilitate process.

Leadership is purposeful influence. It is creating an atmosphere where people rekindle desire and become willing to utilize their strengths. Leadership is taking people someplace good where they have never been before, but they believe is better than where they are now. It is knowing that we are much more than what we see on the outside — and believing in the potential we each possess on the inside. It is about creating workplaces that trust and honor and encourage so the fullness of who we are can be expressed. Leaders understand that without effective, motivated people, tasks and job descriptions won't be completed as effectively as they could be and businesses can't be as successful as they could be.

This clearly suggests that the leader today must understand the key role of relationships and how to build them, because the *strength* of an organization will be determined by the relationships. Power does not come from one individual. It comes from the quality of the relationships and the flow of process as a result of the relationships. This will certainly require greater skills in listening, communicating, facilitating, etc. Individuals who relate to self-power, coercive behavior, and autocratic behavior, and who do not sincerely

care for others in the business, create negative energy re-
sulting in low morale, loss of enthusiasm, absenteeism, and
ultimately turnover.

More effectively building the relationships necessary to accomplish what we want requires a few guiding principles more so
than rules, regulations, and strict policies. It is the principles,
the deeply rooted values, the guiding vision, and as a result,
the organization's culture that will be a strong influence to
shape the behavior of every team member, and hence the
organization. It is the leader's responsibility to communicate
them clearly and insure that they are ever present. The
stringent rules and structures of the past give way to a new
order — one that empowers individuals to act within their
understanding of the concepts and principles of the vision
and values. Where people believe in and support these
principles, you'll find a business that flows, that is life-
giving and energizing, rather than draining, de-motivating,
de-energizing, and stagnant.

Leadership isn't a title — and it isn't a passive process. It requires that we be willing to build the team members. It requires that we be willing to step out of the comfort zone to risk
and change in order to grow. It is understanding that the
world is moving too fast to stay with what we've always done,
even though it may have worked well in the past. Good leaders know that if they try to maintain what has always been,
they will inevitably begin the process of decline and eventually go the way of the horse and buggy. The three questions
leaders continually ask are, "Where are we headed?" "How
will we get there?" and "How are we doing?"

It is important to understand, too, that leadership isn't all
black and white. It isn't even all facts, but includes much

intuition as well. The leader of today must remain flexible, and be open to new information, both internally and externally, and process data with continually growing levels of self-awareness and a willingness and strong ability to reflect. An organization that will stay open to communication and actively develop a strong identity is one that is less subject to change forced from the outside.

Great leaders see things when others can't, or before they do. Sometimes it means making changes and moving ahead before others know what is happening. They must be able to see the forest *and* the trees, to have the ability to step back from what is happening at the moment and see where they are, where people have been, and where they are headed. It is understanding resources which include people, money, raw materials and technology, and understanding that people are the very most important, and greatest, asset. Leaders sense what is happening among their people. They are tuned in to their hopes and fears and concerns. And leaders can see and acknowledge their own strengths, weaknesses, skills, and current state of mind. They must be sincere not only in dealing with others, but in dealing with themselves.

Finally, leadership isn't a "safe harbor" where you get to a certain place and can maintain the status quo forever. That might be an ideal dream, but that's not leadership, nor is it the world in which we live. Leaders must ask questions — and continue to ask questions. They must *rock* the boat, *allow* the boat to rock and *keep things rocked* until they come to a new understanding and level of efficiency. The effective leaders of the 21st century must not fear that chaos will result when they give themselves a new freedom to see what is around (or around the corner), to be open to new information, and to communicate that to their people. It is precisely these elements that will, when the vision is clear and you know who and what you stand for in your organization, provide you both creativity and boundaries, the power to evolve and yet to remain consistent with your values, to be a team player and at the same time allow the individual to blossom within that team.

Perhaps more than at any other time in history, to be really successful, a business must be like a symphony — and the leader is the director. Each person must utilize his or her strengths and capabilities to play a distinct part on their own instruments while playing the same song. The leader must be able to see the big picture, because it is the leader who ultimately chooses the song, sets the pace, and identifies the key in which it will be sung. The symphony is the result of the whole that is created — *and that's the only music that will be heard.*

The Impact of Inspired Vision

"Where are we headed?" "How will we get there?" and "How are we doing?" are questions raised in the last chapter on leadership, and getting there requires vision.

A vision provides a reference point and a mental model of the business you want in the future. It answers the question, "What do we want to create?" It focuses on the longer term orientation and provides a reason for continued growth. It sets the standards of excellence and reflects the high ideals of your business. A truly powerful vision can make an incredible difference in you, your life, and the lives of the people you lead.

The process of visioning lays the foundation to break through self-imposed barriers about what you have done and how you have done it, and move forward with what you can do and how you can do it. It is about having a sense of what is possible, and seeing what others don't necessarily see (an important ability for leaders). It challenges you to look at your business in new ways. What is it that you do? Who are your customers? What are the basic assumptions from which you operate? What internal processes, techniques, systems and operations reinforce your values? Identifying and developing a vision involves sorting through lots of ideas, speculations, desires, assumptions, and certainly value judgments. In fact, the vision follows from your values. If it is your business, it

follows from your values. If it is someone else's
business,your values must line up with the company vision
in order to have a successful partnership and one that will
be comfortable and enjoyed.

The greatest inspiration you can provide to people, as their
leader, is the power of your conviction about your vision. And
the vision that comes alive is the one you are passionate about.
As you see the bigger picture and share it with your employees or team, each person is encouraged and stimulated. When
the vision takes hold within you, you will begin to move in the
direction of that vision. A clearly-articulated and communicated vision helps team members feel like an integral part of
the business rather than simply doing a job that is only one
piece of the puzzle. It builds energy and enthusiasm among
the team members because of *your* passion and enthusiasm. As
the energy builds they will begin to feel a sense of responsibility to do their parts in building the organization, as well as a
sense of responsibility for how the entire team functions, not
just for their own jobs. Challenges, obstacles, and problems
along the way don't become overwhelming because the passion for the vision is stronger, and carries the individuals to
overcome them. When a team is committed to a powerful,
clearly-communicated and understood vision, they will go the
extra mile and take extraordinary steps to turn it into reality.

The vision provides the backbone for everything else that
happens in the organization. Once people are committed to a
vision, they will abandon old ways of thinking, old paradigms
that get in the way of achievement. With a powerful vision
and a committed leader, people change. And when people
change, things change! A dynamic vision keeps both the leader
and the team focused on the goals and objectives during the

good times and the not so good. *A vision requires risk-taking, that's what leadership is all about.* Everyone involved knows *why* they are doing *what* they are doing when the vision is clear.

Leaders truly are the visionaries. They are required to be. But where does the vision comes from? A vision is intrinsic. It comes from deep within you, from your passion. It is the very best of you. It is something you strongly feel, believe and desire. It isn't something you create out of nothing. It already exists inside you, waiting to be uncovered, identified, brought to the surface and lived out. It answers the question of what? What do you want to create? What do you want your business (or family or relationships) to look like? Everything should be considered — the kind of team you employ, the product or service you deliver, how you treat and relate to the customer. Write it out. Take the time to think it through (and it will take some time). Be clear about where you are headed. Know what it is you want to create. And then, and only then, will you be able to lead the people you employ to help you get where you want to go. The vision is a target. It gives everyone a clear understanding of what you are trying to build or create.

A clearly-defined vision is critical because it gives the foundation for every decision you make in the business. You see, from the vision stems the mission which answers the question of why. Why do we do what we do on a daily basis? And then from that arises another question of values. How do we *do* what we do? How do we operate, treat people (each other, customers, suppliers, etc.)? The values are your guiding light as to how you go about doing what you do. A vision begins and ends with values, your values begin the vision and ultimately define the values of the organization and how you operate within that organization.

With vision, mission, and values clearly identified, the other
decisions along the way are much easier to make. The vision,
mission, and values provide the target, always telling you
where to direct your action. Whenever you have a decision to
make, you simply hold that situation up against your vision
and ask what you need to do to stay in line with your vision,
mission, and values. It makes the day-to-day operations, and
the overseeing of employees, so much easier because you
already have your measuring rod. Obviously, this implies
that when you hire an individual that person must be fully
accepting of the vision, mission, and the values within
which they must work. When you stick with it and use this
as your benchmark or measuring rod, you'll find life much
easier. If you don't stay in line with your vision, mission,
and values, you'll find yourself creating a great deal of
needless stress and cognitive dissonance by believing one
thing, but living out another.

As you determine your vision, remember that the only way to
be happy and fulfilled in any business (or anything else in life,
for that matter) is to be yourself, and to be your best self. Don't
try to become someone else. That doesn't mean you don't
grow and progress, but it does mean that you don't do something just because somebody else does it, or to keep up with
the person next door. Your vision must be consistent with your
values. A vision that is not consistent with values will fail to
inspire or motivate (you or anyone else) and may actually
create or engender cynicism. No one can be truly happy or
sincerely enjoy his or her vocation, regardless of what it is, if
personal values are violated. Although we may look to various outside factors to bring fulfillment, when we learn that it
comes from the inside, we have made a great discovery.

Because we live in a dynamic world, our vision must be dynamic, not static. As you travel further down the road, your vision may take on a different look. And that's perfectly okay. In fact, the vision should be revisited on a regular basis to make sure it is still in line with your thinking and aspirations. Your vision is a part of an ongoing *process* of keeping your business up-to-date and integrated with the changes in the outside world as new realities emerge. It is with the values, vision and mission as the blueprint that you can stand strong in the face of change. It is having a changeless core of values on the inside that will allow you the freedom and the ability to change in these times of rapid transformation. If these are not clear, and the winds of change blow strong, you may find yourself grasping for the next move.

Remember that there is no one big step to success. It is one small step in the right direction, followed by the next, and then the next. That will get you to where you want to go, as long as you are clear about where you are headed.

Make sure you live, personally and professionally, so you don't compromise your values. Satisfaction will follow, and with it success, *your style,* following right on its heels. Quality in leadership and business is related to the fulfillment of your purpose, and to the lives you touch. And one of those lives is yours!

Be Smart About Your Health

Why is it that so many give lip service to the idea that "if you've lost your health you've lost everything," then go on living as though it will take care of itself or act as though they are indestructible? Why is it we talk about how important it is, then do very little about it? Lest you say we are living in a time in the United States of much greater awareness about health, why then are hundreds of thousands of people dying every year from heart disease, stroke, cancer, complications of diabetes, effects of obesity, and on and on?

Did you know that heart disease, our number one killer in the United States today, is a relatively new disease? The first modern cases of it were reported in 1912, and even then it was extremely rare. And what about cancer? Only 3% of us died of cancer one hundred years ago. Today almost one in three, or 30%, succumb to it. And stroke, our number three killer, killed very few a hundred years ago. The World Health Organization reports that 50% of annual deaths–24.5 million people worldwide, are victims of cancer, heart and lung disease. What is going on? Obviously something has gone terribly wrong. Sadly, many people consider these diseases a normal part of the aging process. There is nothing normal about degenerative disease. In fact, many of these deaths are totally unnecessary.

These major killers are all diet related. That means we have a great amount of control over them if we would just follow the principles that gain and maintain health. Perhaps the answer lies in a principle that is at the root of many other issues: commitment and discipline — or lack of either.

This book is about success and it pretty much requires that we are healthy in order do to what is necessary to achieve success in any area of life. Because space is limited, it isn't the purpose of this chapter to cover in depth each of the issues involved and how to go about dealing with each one. Rather, it is written to increase your awareness of the areas where attention needs to be given to maintain or regain health.

What many people experience today isn't full blown disease as we have generally come to think of disease, but it isn't great health, either. The lack of a diagnosed or named disease doesn't spell health. Many people are plagued by headaches, skin problems, allergies, stiffness and sore joints, chronic fatigue, insomnia, lack of endurance, regular colds or flu, blood sugar imbalances, and a whole host of other issues. You name it. The list could go on and it doesn't add up to good health.

The list of factors for good health that requires our attention is not long. But what is on the list is important to pay attention to if we truly desire to stay healthy, feel good, and have the energy we would like to have to go through life.

There is no cure as good as prevention. Any health program should have as its thesis the anticipation and prevention of disease rather than its mere identification and treatment. But that's not what is happening with the majority of individuals in our country.

For many, health remains a mystery. The effort becomes one of
trying to solve problems. It is really quite simple, but it is not
easy. The age-old principle of reaping what we sow is so true
in our health but because the reaping, the results, often comes
so many years later in the form of disease, we don't get the
connection. Or perhaps we have known for some time of our
depleting habits, and we want things to be different, but we
just don't want to make the changes necessary to regain or
retain good health.

Isn't it interesting that when an airplane crashes and a few
hundred people die it makes headline news — and not only for
one day, but for weeks, even months and sometimes even for
years! But when a million people die of heart disease or a half
million people die of cancer, doesn't it seem strange that we're
not giving it the same attention? Get this: The number of
people dying from heart disease is equivalent to a jumbo jet
full of people crashing every single hour of every single day of
every single month for an entire year — year, after year, after
year! It's time to wake up. We think we have a safety net at
the end of the dead end road ahead — but it's not there. Instead, when we get there we'll find all that is left is a steep cliff
or a sudden fall — unless we begin making important changes
today.

Certainly, we will all die a physical death at some point. But
that does not mean we must encourage the process or speed it
up as we travel through this lifetime. Many people take better
care of their cars than they do of their bodies, purchasing the
most expensive products to take care of them. They take more
time planning their vacations; and spend more hours watching television programs that fill the mind with untruths, outright lies and deception, than they even begin to take in caring
for their health.

There is good news, however. We can rebuild our bodies and we have done that from the time we were born. Howard University tells us that our bodies are rebuilt every two years, and that 98% of a body can be rebuilt in one year. For example: We are told that we rebuild a new brain in one year; the bloodstream every 4 months; the stomach lining every 5 days; the skeleton every 3 months; the liver every 6 weeks; the kidneys every 2 months; and the skin every month! This is awesome. But we must also realize that if we have a liver that has degenerated and is very unhealthy, let's say we give it a grade of a "D" — it will not rebuild the next time around to an "A" no matter how much we change our lifestyle, nutrition, etc. It will become progressively better over time — but not all at once. It took time to create the problem — and it will take some time to reverse it as well.

General health and well-being is obtained by our lifestyles: what we eat, what we drink, how we think, and the exercise we get. It is short sighted to believe we have a single problem and that we simply need to take a pill or medication or have a surgery performed to fix it. The entire body works as a whole and when it is not cleansed (toxins eliminated) and nourished (proper nutrients provided, then digested and assimilated), "symptoms" develop. These symptoms are the deterioration of our bodies in our weakest spots. Continuing to do the same thing we are doing today will only cause deterioration at a greater level down the road. Unless we are willing to change, we may get the result we *never* hoped or prayed for.

It's Time to Wake Up
Few would argue today that our food and lifestyles, at least those of the majority of the population, are slowly undermining us — our health and vitality. We are seeing newly identified diseases, new syndromes, earlier onset of problems that used to be called "old age problems." Glance at most any obituary

column in the paper and you'll find causes for death like "died of heart attack, age 42," "died of cancer, age 32," or "died of complications of diabetes, age 35." Furthermore, the United States Public Health Service says seven of ten Americans over the age of 40 have a chronic disease.

Although we understand that it typically takes a long time to develop a chronic, degenerative disease, we're seeing these same diseases at a much earlier age. We truly are, by our food and lifestyles, working against ourselves. A muscular dystrophy campaign motto has been, "Your change is the key to a cure." Very true. When it comes to our health, change of a different sort is the key not only to the cure — but to prevention — and perhaps more important, to living a life with vitality.

Heredity

Before we move further, let's quickly review a little about heredity. Our genetic composition, received from our parents (and thus from our grandparents, great-grandparents, etc.), determines who we are at birth. If a parent had heart problems, or any other organs that were weak, we may tend to have similar problems. We know that a history of weakness in the family often means we should take extra care of our health regarding that area. Although we may have inherited tendencies for particular weaknesses, they can remain tendencies and not result in actual problems if we take care of ourselves. It is what we do and how we live that will determine how we are affected.

A Greater Perspective

It is important that we understand that care must be taken of the whole body including all the various organs. They are capable of working in perfect harmony, which gives us optimal function. When any one of the body systems or organs is not functioning properly, the entire body suffers. This means we must look at the whole person, not only the physical body, but attitudes and emotions as well. A greater, or wholistic, perspective includes physical, mental/emotional and spiritual. It involves, quite simply, how we live.

Physical
Physically we consider nutrition, exercise, and breathing. Each of these is important to total health. Many, if not most, current-day Americans are living in the fast lane and are practically committing suicide on the installment plan with their unhealthy diets and lack of exercise.

Nutrition. Most everyone would agree somewhat with the statement, "We are what we eat." How we eat is a significant part of our health. By eating the good food God has provided, we strengthen the organs of the body and provide our physical structure with necessary nutrients. Refined, processed and sugar-laden foods are taking their toll. Meat and dairy, although we have been "sold a bill of goods" that we need these in our diet, are totally unnecessary and, instead, are doing a great deal of harm. Interestingly, in countries where people eat little or no meat or dairy products, the incidence of health issues like osteoporosis and obesity are nearly unknown. It is not yet widely understood that diets high in protein, most notably animal protein (including dairy) cause calicum to be depleted from our systems. The high protein content of meat and dairy actually depletes our bodies of calcium, rather than providing calcium. Actually, then, maintaining strong bones depends more on preventing calcium loss than on increasing calcium intake.

We would do well to eat from around the perimeter of the
grocery store. That means more from the produce section and
less from the interior. What do you find in the interior of the
grocery store? Here's where the packaged, processed, and
refined products are boxed, plastic wrapped, canned, etc. A
healthy diet of raw foods supplies much more oxygen, enzymes, and nutrients. In fact, enzymes are gone from the
processed and cooked foods we eat. Concentrating on fruits,
vegetables, seeds, nuts, grains, and legumes is a much
healthier choice. These are natural foods that strengthen the
body, nourish weak organs, and help to eliminate waste matter from the body.

We cannot mention nutrition and the physical part of our well-
being without also pointing out the absolute necessity of
water. We all know that we can live for days without food, but
not long without water. The best water to drink is either
distilled or purified and we should be consuming, as a rule of
thumb, approximately one ounce of water for every two
pounds of body weight. When you get into the higher weight
ranges, this is moderated a bit. The old standby of eight
glasses of water a day is still appropriate—and a good start as
a minimum. Our bodies are mostly water and without it, we
cannot flush the toxins efficiently. When this occurs, waste and
toxins (even from the normal metabolism of our cells) build up
in the system and will eventually create problems.

Exercise. If diet were the only key to good health, then every
vegan would be the picture of great health. But this simply is
not true. Optimum health requires that we must exercise too.
One of the important needs of the body is that it move. We
hear "use it or lose it" applied to many things—and this ap-
plies to our bodies as well. A growing epidemic of obesity in
our Western society is one result of the sedentary lifestyle

many live. Adults, and children as well, spend less time moving their bodies than at any time in history, and we are suffering the results in the incidence of heart disease, high blood pressure, diabetes, arthritis, osteoporosis, and cancer. Exercise can also alter many of the typical markers of aging such as bone density, aerobic capacity, muscle mass, strength, and even mental well-being.

Regular exercise is essential to good health. This doesn't require belonging to some athletic organization or maintaining a membership to the local workout gym. Fast walking costs nothing except your time and commitment. Even when the weather is bad you can move your walking indoors. Shopping malls are a popular alternative that costs you nothing. Many malls nationwide let walkers in before shopping hours, often between the hours of 6:30 A.M. and 10 A.M. Walking thirty to forty minutes a day does miracles for your body. Particular disciplines, such as Yoga, are wonderful for stretching and flexibility, two other important factors in our physical health.

Breathing. Perhaps you've never considered breathing an exercise, but whatever you call it, it is very important to your health. Obviously, you are breathing or you wouldn't be alive. But do you breathe deeply and fully? Many people are literally oxygen-starving their bodies by their shallow breathing, or holding of breath. Proper breathing, when it becomes a habit, will regenerate the cells of our bodies. It will also help us to relax. We'll probably find that we sleep better too. The entire body will be rejuvenated, including our minds. Our digestion and elimination will be enhanced from proper breathing as well.

As you consider exercising for yourself, be sure to keep in mind that a complete program includes stretching, strength training and cardiovascular conditioning. Typical rules of thumb include 30 minutes of aerobic activity at least three times a week and 20 minutes of strength training at least three times a week. Consider beginning each exercise period with several minutes of stretching to increase and maintain flexibility, as well as preparing you for the rest of your workout.

If you haven't been in the habit of making exercise a part of your daily routine, it will take discipline to get yourself going — to gain momentum and then to stay there. But it will do wonders for you in every area of your life. It's always hardest getting started — but once you do, and after you've developed the habit of including this regularly — I can just about guarantee you that you will not want to set it aside so easily the next time you are tempted. The rewards are very evident to those who develop the discipline to exercise regularly.

Mental/Emotional

This has to do with how you think and feel, and includes your attitude, how much stress you feel and how you deal with it. Actually, our worldview has a lot to do with how we feel. It is how we perceive those events around us that determines, to a great extent, how they affect us. Our minds are incredible and they play such a significant part in our overall health. It has been said that every word you say is communicated to the body — and the physical body actually responds. Tell yourself long enough that you are sick and you will actually become sick.

Stress, even when not the cause of physical symptoms or ailments, often aggravates conditions. It has a powerful effect because of what it does in the body. Very simply stated, when we are under stress the body is flooded with adrenaline and other hormones, and the nervous system reactions are heightened. The heart pumps faster, and blood rushes to various parts of the body—all in a matter of a few seconds.

Today's adrenal alarm goes off for much different reasons that the fight or flight of days gone by: traffic jams, computer crashes, angry bosses, washing machine overflows, family squabbles. You name it. Our adrenal glands are controlled by the nervous system and are responsible for pumping out adrenaline in response to stress, excitement, or anxiety. After a continued period of time the constant stress overworks these glands and they become exhausted. The consequences can be far-reaching because there is hardly a system in the body that is not influenced either directly or indirectly by adrenal activity. And when this happens you and your body do not respond to life in the same way as you would to the same stressors before the results had built up in your body.

Stress itself, however, is not the villain. It is *how we respond* to it that is more important. Those who feel negative about the stress will find it takes a greater toll than those who understand the reason for the stress and are willing to deal with it in order to accomplish a certain task or function. It is important to understand, too, that stimulants such as coffee, tobacco, drugs, etc., and even sugar, can intensify the negative results of stress.

More than ever before, as the pace of life accelerates, we need times of calm, uninterrupted moments for the renewal they can bring to our bodies and spirit.

Spiritual

People today, as in the past, are seeking for something beyond themselves. They want to make a difference, they want life to have meaning. In fact, a good part of the reason people strive

so hard to become a "success" is because they simply haven't
yet understood that success is far more than titles, bank accounts, investment portfolios, and material goods. There is a
deeper meaning that can be filled only when one comes to
terms with his or her Creator; when we can finally answer the
questions: Why am I here? And what is my purpose?

Without coming to an understanding within as to what this
means in our lives, we push ourselves to the limits trying to
find that thing, that position, that person, that job, that whatever—that will make us feel complete or whole. We will search
everywhere to find a place of peace and contentment—and it
simply will not be found in material goods. Only when one
comes to terms with this will he or she be able to come to
terms with life, including relationships, vocation, and indeed,
everything that comprises this life.

We need to get very clear about what is really important to us,
what we really want, and then live by the principles that will
assure we are headed in the right direction. Then, and only
then, will we know what true success is. Then, and only then,
will we know the thrill, the satisfaction, and the fulfillment of
life at its best, personally and professionally, because we will
have come to understand that it isn't about "us" or "me" at all.

Pulling it all together

Just as our health is determined by heredity, what we eat,
what we drink, and how we think and feel, so too is it im-
pacted by our lifestyles. Everything we do has an effect upon
our health. Are you paying attention to what you eat and the
nutrients required by your body? Are you getting enough
exercise? Do you breathe completely and fully? Do you take
time out to relax and renew, or are you always on the run? Do

you refrain from things that will drain your health, energy and vitality like drugs (legal or illegal), smoking, excessive drinking, pushing yourself too hard, and never taking a break? And how about your attitude? And most importantly, have you really, truly figured out why you are on this earth, and what you are doing here?

Certainly your good health requires some thought, and then a commitment of your attitude, your desire, and your actions. What is truly exciting and can give everyone great hope is that the body can be renewed when you treat the *cause* of malfunction and not simply alleviate its effects (symptoms).

But there is a catch — *no one else can do it for you.* Not even doctors. Certainly, God is all powerful here and we don't truly do the healing ourselves. God provides the healing by giving us bodies created to heal if they are given what they need to do the job, and if they are able to eliminate what they don't want and cannot use. We can't buy health or healing. It must be earned by our own discipline and change of habits. Remember — it's your choice!

Keeping
The Flame
Alive

Al Siebert, Ph.D.

Mastering the Five Levels of Resilience

Resilience is essential in today's world. To remain healthy and cope well in this era of non-stop change, you must be able to deal with unexpected challenges and overcome adversities. In the workplace, very few people have up-to-date job descriptions. Some corporations have stopped providing job descriptions altogether. Large organizations, to remain competitive, have eliminated most middle management positions and laid off many workers. Employees now work with less supervision in self-directed, culturally diverse work teams. Workers are expected to learn and master new technology very quickly. Everyone feels pressured to get more work done, of higher quality, with fewer people, in less time, with less budget.

Highly resilient people are change-proficient. They know how to bounce back from setbacks and find a way to have things turn out well. They thrive in non-stop change because they are optimistic, flexible, and creative. They learn from experience and are synergistic. They handle major difficulties better than most people because they know how to gain strength from adversity. When hit by major setbacks they don't complain about life being unfair. Like cats, they manage to land on their feet and often end up stronger and better than before.

People best suited for constant change are different from people suited for unchanging conditions. A production manager says, "It used to be that when you worked harder, took work home, worked extra hours, and took evening classes, you were aiming for a promotion. Now it means that you might be able to keep your job another six months."

Pride in one's work can be hard to maintain when old ways of doing things are discarded. A project engineer said, "It was hard to be enthusiastic and fully committed to the new project after management discarded a system I devoted years to developing."

Morale is a problem when friendships with coworkers are disrupted by reorganization and layoffs. All of these challenges and more help explain why information about how to be resilient is a high priority in today's world.

People react to disruptive change and setbacks in different ways. Some people explode into angry action. They have an emotional tantrum toward others and may express the desire to hurt someone.

Some people do the opposite. They implode. They go numb. They feel helpless and cannot express their feelings. They feel so overwhelmed they can't even try to cope with what has happened.

Emotionally healthy people let themselves feel upset. They verbalize their feelings, then reorient and develop plans for coping and recovering from what has happened.

Some people portray themselves as victims. They blame others for ruining their lives. They become mired in unhappy thoughts and feelings. They complain over and over, "This isn't fair!" "Ain't it awful." "Look what they've done to me now."

Sadly, some people get stuck in the victim/blaming mode.
They reject all suggestions on how to cope with what has
happened. They never take steps to overcome their difficulties,
even when the crisis is over. The victim reaction to adversity
undercuts one's ability to handle unexpected change effectively. Getting stuck in this frame of mind is like tying a rope
around your feet and then trying to run a race—it's a major
handicap. The victim response is devastating because it makes
you feel helpless, has you blaming others for your bad situation, and places responsibility on others for making things
better for you.

Research by Martin Seligman and other psychologists shows
that believing you are helpless and hopeless is far more harm-
ful than the actual events that contribute to those feelings. No
matter how rotten the situation may be, you simply can't
afford to think, feel, or behave like a victim. The five-level
action plan that follows will show you how to get yourself out
of the victim/blaming mode. You can't just make your feelings
go away of course, but you can move through them. You can
handle them in such a way that they won't prevent you from
getting your life back on track.

Highly resilient survivors have a coping/learning reaction
when hit with unexpected disruptions, no matter how unfair.
When hurt and distressed they expect to bounce back and find
a way to have things turn out well. They thrive in constant
change because they are flexible, agile, creative, adapt quickly,
are synergistic, and learn from experience. They handle major
difficulties better than most people because they know how to
gain strength from adversity. When hit by major setbacks they
don't complain about life being unfair. Like cats, they manage
to land on their feet when the bottom drops out of their lives
and often end up stronger and better than before.

Fortunately, you were born with the potential to develop these abilities. The five-level resiliency plan shows how to do that.

1. Maintain Your Emotional Stability, Health, and
   Well-Being
2. Focus Outward: Good Problem Solving Skills
3. Focus Inward: Develop Strong Inner "Selfs"
4. Develop High Level Resiliency Skills
5. Develop the Talent for Serendipity

The first level is essential to sustaining your health, your energy, and positive feelings.

The second level focuses outward on the challenges that must be handled; it is based on research findings that problem-focused coping leads to resiliency better than emotion-focused coping.

The third level focuses inward on the roots of resiliency — strong self-esteem, self-confidence, and a positive self-concept. These three core "selfs" are like gatekeepers to your higher level abilities.

At the fourth level you fully develop the attributes and skills found in highly resilient people (indicated by a high score on the Resiliency Quiz).

The fifth level is the highest level of resiliency. It is the talent for serendipity — the ability to convert misfortune into good fortune.

When faced with adversity, it is useful to remember that:

- Your mind and habits will create either barriers or bridges to a better future. Positive emotions broaden and build your resiliency strengths. Negative emotions limit and weaken your resiliency.

- Resiliency can't be taught, but it can be learned. It comes from working to develop and strengthen your unique combination of inborn abilities.

- The struggle to bounce back and recover from setbacks can lead to developing strengths and abilities that you didn't know were possible.

Resiliency comes from discovering and developing a deep emotional wisdom about yourself and other people. It comes from learning how to handle the processes of transformation when your life is disrupted. Resiliency comes to you as you learn how easy life becomes when you focus your energies and your intentions on having things work well for everyone.

Maintain Your Emotional Stability, Health, and Well-Being

The Motorola Corporation, in its resiliency workshops for employees, defined resiliency as "the ability to absorb high levels of disruptive change while displaying minimal dysfunctional behavior." Everyone hit with disruptive change goes through a period of emotional turmoil. Resilient people handle their emotional reactions in healthy ways and do not add to the coping challenges of others by acting in dysfunctional ways.

Disruptions in the workplace are so frequent and deep in today's organizations, it is no longer sufficient to think of *stress reduction*, *adapting*, or *adjusting*. The following method for sustaining your spirit has proven to be of great value to thousands of people. Getting caught up in a victim/blaming mode is devastating because it makes you feel helpless. It creates thoughts and feelings of being a helpless victim in a hopeless situation where other people and events have control over your life and your future.

To maintain your vitality during times of adversity, the following "Health-Sustaining Action Plan" will be very effective.

Part One: The first part of the Health-Sustaining Plan is to make two lists. In one list you will write down everything in your life that you experience as emotionally draining, unpleasant, and have negative or unhappy feelings about. In the second list you will write down what you experience as pleasant, positive, and revitalizing. Writing these two lists will immediately lead to a much better feeling of control over your life.

The second part of the Health-Sustaining Plan will be to take actions to decrease your negative experiences and increase your positive experiences. We'll get to that in a few minutes.

I've taught this Health-Sustaining Plan to thousands of people. When you make this plan your own, you will experience many benefits. You will feel in control of your life and learn how to create a positive, supportive environment for yourself.

Healthy people will express their unhappy feelings as a step toward regaining a positive frame of mind. If you were raised to be a "good child" who is always happy and never complains, writing this list may be hard to do. The handicapping effects of "good child" habits will become more apparent as we go along. For now, however, give yourself emergency permission to write about your distress and the things that drain your energy.

The Negative List: What Upsets You?

Make a long list of everything you feel upset and distressed about. Include anything in your life that drains your energy. Spend time writing how you feel about what you put on your list.

Resist getting swept up in strong group feelings. Those
feelings can inhibit your ability to reorient to the new reality. While it is important to acknowledge your genuine
feelings, it is also important that you protect your ability to
bounce back by consciously deciding not be drawn into the
litany of grievances coming from co-workers. If you have
sorted through your personal feelings, you will be less
susceptible to the pull of group emotions.

Research by psychologist James Pennebaker shows that
people cope better with disruptive change when they write
about their deepest feelings. Be specific. Here are some
examples: "I feel very angry that I had to bump my co-
worker. I feel afraid that I may lose my paycheck and not be
able to make my mortgage payments." Statements such as
"the bumping is inhumane" or "the reorganization is stupid" are not saying how you feel. Just keep saying over and
over "I feel because..." "I feel angry about..." and so forth.
Unexpressed feelings can drain your energy when you need
it most.

Talk With a Friend
Tell a friend what you are feeling. A friend will listen, sym-
pathize, and won't tell you not to feel what you are feeling.
Be sure to tell your friend what you want from him or her.
If you want your friend just to listen and not problem solve
while you unload, let him or her know. If you want some
suggestions and coaching on what to do, let your friend
know that. Let friends know what you need.

Stress research shows that people who do not cope well
usually feel isolated. They have no close friends to talk to,
or spend time with. Remember: A burden that is shared is
not as heavy.

Ask Others for Help and Support
If you have always been the strong one in the family, now is
the time to ask your spouse, your children, and perhaps
even your brothers or sisters for emotional support and
encouragement. If it is unusual for you to be the one who
needs emotional support, they will probably love you all the
more. They may have been tired of you always being the
person who helps others.

Be sure to consider seeing a counselor provided by the
Employee Assistance Program. It is already paid for, and
could be very helpful at this time.

The Positive List: What Revitalizes You?
What do you enjoy doing the most? Each of us has experiences that renew us. Examples might be watching comedy
videotapes, listening to music, gardening, hiking, spending
time with pets, playing a musical instrument, playing with
children, or recreational reading.

Make a list of activities that revitalize you and help
you sleep well. After listing the activities that revitalize and nourish you, make sure you do some of
them!

Don't neglect pleasant activities when you are under pressure. The human spirit requires nourishment.

Psychiatrist William Glasser interviewed dozens of people
who held up well under extreme pressure to find out how
they avoided "burnout." He found that most of them had a
"positive addiction." They had a favorite activity, such as

bike riding or jogging, that they always did no matter what. The lesson: It is essential for your emotional survival and well-being to do what is good for you.

Part Two: Reduce Energy-Draining Experiences, Increase Positive Experiences, Decrease Your Negative Experiences

The survivor resiliency research shows that resilient people rarely feel helpless or hopeless. They feel hopeful and cope with difficulties in active, problem-solving ways. When struggling with a rough situation, they focus their energies on finding ways to take control of what is happening.

Look at your list of what upsets you or drains your energy. Look at each item and ask yourself, "What can I do about this?"

Your options may include:

- Choose not to waste mental or emotional energy on matters totally out of your control.

- Pick one upsetting item and develop a plan for changing it. You might decrease your contact with it. That is, make it stay away from you. Or you could stay away from it (such as going for a walk at noon instead of listening to all the negative talk in the lunch room). If someone starts to tell you what he or she is upset about without asking your permission, ask him or her to stop. You might say "Please, I can't handle hearing that right now."

- Decide to stop being upset. Accept that what is happening in your organization is the new way of life. A survivor tip: Act as though this is exactly what you wanted! Choose to have it happen.

- Become an observer. Watch what is happening with curiosity.

- During a period of turmoil, create a new coping plan every day. Ask "What must I do to get through to-day?"

- Develop contingency plans. For each possible development have two plans, Plan A and Plan B. Think them through. This will help you relax during the uncertainty, and you will be instantly ready to act in a positive way no matter what happens.

Remember: It isn't the situation that counts, it is how you react to situations that determines your future.

Increase Your Positive Experiences
Efforts to decrease your negative experiences are only one-half of your action plan. Increasing your positive experiences is very important, and is actually *more* important than decreasing your negative experiences. Pleasant, positive experiences revitalize you, boost your immunity to emotional toxicity, and give you more strength to sustain yourself in adverse circumstances.

If you were raised *never* to be selfish, now is a good time to question that childhood prohibition. Taking good care of yourself does not mean you are a selfish person. For your health and well-being, it is essential to include yourself on the list of people you do good things for.

Look at your list of what revitalizes you.

- Ask questions about how to repeat, increase, or have new positive experiences.

- Develop a plan of action for increasing positive, revitalizing experiences.

Do what renews you and lets you sleep better. Examples might be time with friends, watching recordings of comedy shows, listening to music, dancing, bike riding, time with pets, playing a musical instrument, athletic activities, taking naps, or reading. Don't neglect pleasant activities when you are under pressure.

Remember: *It is essential for your emotional survival and well-being to do what is good for you.*

Your Health-Sustaining Plan for *decreasing* distressing experiences and *increasing* revitalizing ones will keep you from feeling helpless and hopeless. It will strengthen your emotional immunity to events that could be distressing, and increase your resiliency.

Another benefit is that the better you become at holding up under pressure, the more you can help others cope well. You can do this by asking someone that you care about these two questions: "How are you feeling about what is happening?" and "What are you doing to take care of yourself?" When you ask these two questions and take time to listen, the people you care about will feel better and cope better. Try it the next chance you get. See what happens.

The more that you learn how to consciously *respond* to events in ways that work for you, instead of *reacting* and then blaming others for your reactions, the more you become free to live a life that you enjoy.

When you express your feelings and take good care of yourself, you avoid feeling helpless and hopeless and you have more energy for handling the challenges you face.

References:

Positive Addiction, by William Glasser, M.D.

Opening Up: The Healing Power of Expressing Emotions, by James Pennebaker, Ph.D.

(Note: If you have lost your job, download and follow the steps in the file "How to Handle the Emotional Side of Job Loss and Job Search" at the ResiliencyCenter.com web site.)

Strengthen Your Inner "Selfs"

For many people the main obstacles to effective coping are not in the outside world, they are internal. A crisis such as having your job restructured or losing your job through no fault of your own can expose inner weaknesses that were not obvious in a protected environment. Your struggle to bounce back, however, can lead you to discover strengths you did not know you had. A benefit for many people is finding that their emotional health and stability increase when they break free from old emotional habits.

Something that disrupts your life can make you feel vulnerable. Life-disrupting events that require you to manage your own survival can force you to discover and develop better inner resources. Now is the time to draw upon three powerful inner resources: self-confidence, self-esteem, and self-concept.

When your self-confidence, self-esteem, and self-concept are strong, positive, and healthy, you can cope well with life's challenges. If these inner resources are not strong, however, you tend to be more vulnerable, suffer more, and cope less well. Here is what to do:

Strengthen Your Self-Confidence

Self-confidence refers to how well you expect to do in new assignments. It is an action predictor. It is based on your reputation with yourself. People with strong self-confidence know they can count on themselves even more than they can count on anyone else.

People with strong self-confidence expect to overcome adversities and succeed in new activities. If you know such a person arrange to spend time with her or him. Listen to that person's way of explaining what is happening. Benefit from the person's attitudes. Courage and humor in the face of challenges are contagious. They will rub off on you if you associate with survivors.

Memories of past accomplishments and awareness of your many abilities may not be uppermost in your mind right now, but they need to be!

To increase your self-confidence, make a list of all the things you've done well. Describe what you know you're good at doing. Ask yourself, "What are my reliable strengths and abilities? What do I do well?"

After you have created the list of your reliable strengths, you are going to do something that truly requires courage — practice talking about your strengths to another person. Ask a good friend to help you with this exercise. Practice talking about your reliable strengths.

When you join a work team, it is important that you be able to tell the others what your strengths and abilities are. False modesty may be desirable at social functions, but not in highly effective team members.

With all the position changes and reorganization taking place, the people in every office and department must form new teams quickly. A group of people who all have strong self-confidence can form an effective new work team more rapidly. The first step is to discuss and agree on the most important work that must be done right now. Next, discuss who will do what, in what way, by a certain time. The team needs members who know what their best skills are and who will voluntarily speak up and say "I will take responsibility for such-and-such."

Strengthen Your Self-Esteem

Self-esteem is your emotional opinion of yourself. It is the way you feel about yourself as a person. Self-esteem is like a thick emotional blanket that buffers you from hurtful criticism. Self-esteem makes up the gap between positive feedback you receive from others and what you need to sustain yourself psychologically. Self-esteem also determines how much you learn after something goes wrong. How to develop stronger self-esteem:

> Make a list of all the ways you value yourself
> and feel good about yourself. It is very important
> to be consciously able to appreciate yourself. If
> you feel reluctant to do such a list, this is a sign
> that you really need to do it!

To increase your awareness of the importance of self-esteem, talk with some co-workers about differences you've seen between people with low self-esteem, strong self-esteem, and extreme self-esteem. This helps clarify that no one is suggesting that you become a stuck-up, arrogant, "ego maniac." A person with strong, healthy self-esteem is in between two extremes that don't work well.

Self-appreciation lets you shrug off insensitive comments from others. You can have a comeback ready, almost like having a good return in a tennis match. If someone says the downsizing is "getting rid of the dead wood," you might say: "The layoffs are being handled on the basis of lowest seniority, not competence."

Strengthen Your Self-Concept
Self-concept refers to your idea about who and what you are. Some of your self-concept may have been based upon your job title or income level. While this is relatively normal, you will find it useful to shift away from thinking about yourself as a noun ("I am the Department Manager.") to aspects of your self-concept that are internalized. ("I have excellent managing skills.") Inner attributes that you value will be unchanged by a change in job status or job title.

The new workplace is bewildering and disorienting to workers who were trained by their parents and teachers to act, dress, talk, feel, and think as told. The old way of raising children conditioned them to be obedient employees in large organizations that changed very slowly. If you were an obedient employee who followed your job description, were receptive to performance evaluations, and didn't cause problems for managers, you could eventually expect to be old enough to stay home and still get checks.

In the past, the more desirable employee was like an obedient child who cooperated with being controlled by parental authorities. Now, however, the desirable employee is self-motivated, resilient, has an attitude of professionalism, and can work without a job description. Employers now want people who know how to make themselves useful without waiting to be told what to do. Employers want people who are constantly

learning, adapt quickly, work well with others, and find ways
to be successful in new and ambiguous situations. Fortunately,
we are born with the ability to increase our resiliency and
professionalism throughout our lives.

Make a list contrasting the differences between
people who are professional and those who are
unprofessional.

To increase your inner sense of professionalism even further,
get together with a few co-workers and compare your lists.

A self-concept of professionalism is essential in today's
work world. Remember, the obedient employee of the past,
the worker who waited for instructions on what to do, is
now a dead weight in today's lean, fast-changing, agile
organization. The person best suited for today's workplace
has shifted from reliance on job descriptions, to inner attitudes of professionalism.

This isn't hard work, once you start doing it. Strong self-
confidence, healthy self-esteem, a solid sense of professionalism, and becoming highly resilient, build in small steps over a
period of time. You may have relapses when old habits reap-
pear, but your new, better habits will gradually replace them.
Keep in mind that developing your resiliency is not a new way
of acting designed to replace an old act. Resiliency comes from
a discovered self, not a constructed self. It comes from the
gradual emergence of your unique, inborn abilities. The better
you get, the more of a unique individual you become.

When your three inner "selfs" are solid and strong, they can
hold up well even when others try to weaken them. A reality

of life is that there will always be people who criticize you, call you bad names, try to tear you down, and tell you what you cannot accomplish. Strong gatekeepers protect you from such attacks, and let you move ahead with your life.

Develop High-Level Resiliency Skills

When you are forced to cope with highly disruptive change
and major adversity, you will never be the same again. You
will become stronger or weaker, become either better or bitter.
When you sustain your energy well, are good at solving problems, and strengthen your three inner gatekeepers, you have
the foundation in place for handling even the roughest situations and can emerge with new strengths. As you get better
and better you developexcellent emotional intelligence, are
more healthy, and feel happier.

Before reading further, make two lists. What is the difference
between people who are highly resilient, and people who do
not handle disruptive change or setbacks very well?

After you have written out your own list describing what it
takes to be resilient, take the quiz on the next page, "How
Resilient Are You?"

HOW RESILIENT ARE YOU? *

Rate yourself from 1 to 5 on the following: (1 = very little, 5 = very strong)

☐ Very resilient. Adapt quickly. Good at bouncing back from difficulties.

☐ Optimistic, see difficulties as temporary, expect to overcome them and have things turn out well.

☐ In a crisis I calm myself and focus on taking useful actions.

☐ Good at solving problems logically.

☐ Can think up creative solutions to challenges. Trust intuition.

☐ Feel self-confident, enjoy healthy self-esteem, and have an attitude of professionalism about work.

☐ Curious, ask questions, want to know how things work, experiment.

☐ Playful, find the humor, laugh at self, chuckle.

☐ Constantly learn from experience and from the experiences of others.

☐ Very flexible. Feel comfortable with inner complexity (trusting and cautious, unselfish and selfish, optimistic and pessimistic, etc.)

continue...

☐ Anticipate problems to avoid them and expect the unexpected.

☐ Able to tolerate ambiguity and uncertainty about situations.

☐ Good listener. Good empathy skills."Read" people well. Can adapt to various personality styles. Non-judgmental (even with difficult people).

☐ Able to recover emotionally from losses and setbacks. Can express feelings to others, let go of anger, overcome discouragement, and ask for help.

☐ Very durable, keep on going during tough times. Independent spirit.

☐ Have been made stronger and better by difficult experiences.

☐ Have converted misfortune into good fortune, found an unexpected benefit.

☐ Total

Scoring: 75 or higher — very resilient!
65-75 — better than most
55-65 — slow, but adequate
45-55 — you're struggling
45 or under — seek help!

*Adapted from *The Survivor Personality* by Al Siebert, Copyright © Al Siebert, Ph.D.

How well did you do? Hopefully you will feel validated about many aspects of yourself that you may not have appreciated. The following explanation of the items shows why certain attributes contribute to resiliency and how to develop the ones that you believe would benefit you.

Good at Bouncing Back from Difficulties
This is an overall rating for the entire quiz. It indicates how much you see yourself as being resilient when you need to be.

Expect to Have Things Turn Out Well
Resilient people are optimistic. They usually react to a major threat by saying to themselves "Somehow, some way, I am going to do my best to survive this and make things turn out well." In athletic competitions winners expect to win. What you expect to happen influences your responses. Your expectations create a self-fulfilling prophecy. If you expect a good outcome, your brain spots little events and momentary opportunities that will lead to the good outcome. If you expect a bad outcome your brain will have you thinking, feeling, and acting in ways that make you successful at getting that result.

Keep a Playful Sense of Humor
Humor contributes directly to survival. It lets you play with an upsetting situation. Threats and crises can trigger a person's inborn "fight or flight" response. A strong surge of adrenaline can increase the speed of your muscular reflexes and your muscle strength, but it impairs good problem

solving. That is why laughing or joking during a crisis is very practical!

Laughing reduces tension. The sense of humor shown in James Bond and Jackie Chan movies is typical of people who are best at dealing with emergencies and dicey situations.

The humor is not hostile or hurtful. It is directed toward the situation. The person toys with whatever happens and pokes fun at it. Chances for surviving are increased by the attitude, "I'm bigger than this. I'm going to play with it. This is my toy."

Humorous playing is a way of asking "How does this look from a different point of view? What would happen if I turned it upside down? What if the reverse were true? What unusual things exist here?" By playing and toying with the situation, the person avoids being overwhelmed and at the same time is likely to come up with a way to survive.

How about you? Have you ever been poked in the ribs for muttering a humorous comment during a serious moment? If so, that is a good sign.

Questions Help You Orient to the New Reality
Questions help you "read" new realities rapidly. Questions help you create an accurate mental map of the new terrain. A curious person absorbs information and has a more accurate comprehension of what is going on.

Learn, Learn, Learn
If you look in any psychology textbook you will find that
"Learning" is defined as "a change in behavior that results
from experience." This means that "change" and "learning"
are inseparable. Like an old song says, you can't have one
without the other.

The key to a successful career, therefore, is to be constantly
learning new skills, new information, new methods, new
equipment, and new professional techniques. Highly resilient people are life-long learners.

Learn How to Learn in the School of Life
Some of your most important learning does not occur in the
classroom, it occurs in the school of life. Resilient people
learn good lessons from bad experiences. That is how they
become stronger, smarter, better, and more emotionally
intelligent. Psychologists have identified the following steps
as the way to facilitate self-managed learning:

1. Something happens: an incident, an experience.

2. If it is upsetting, handle your feelings first.

3. Reflect on the experience. Observe it. Mentally replay
   it as if remembering a dream.

4. Put it into words. Write it down in a journal or tell
   someone.

5. Ask "What can I learn from this? What is the lesson
   here?"

6. Ask "Next time, what could I do differently? What
   are my options?"

7. Imagine yourself handling the situation differently, better, and getting a desirable outcome.

8. Rehearse all the ways you will or might handle such a situation again should the opportunity arise.

People stuck in the victim/blaming mode do not learn from unpleasant experiences. That is why they accumulate more and more negative experiences. They dwell on "if only such and such hadn't happened," and are focused backward on the past. They tighten up when faced with a similar situation and do not cope well with the next one either. In contrast, people who dwell on "The next time..." face the future with optimism about the challenges. They expect to do better the next time and usually do.

Be Flexible and Adaptable
Tough challenges may call upon your ability to use both logical reasoning and your intuition. Although these qualities may seem to be contradictory, being able to use both one ability and its opposite can be of tremendous help in doing the right thing at the right time. Don't limit yourself by believing that you have to stick with one personality quality, like always being optimistic. Resilient people have a greater than normal range of responses in critical situations. Combinations of internal, opposing personality qualities give a person choices for taking the best action for a situation.

Here are some of the contradictory or paradoxical personality qualities observed in life's best survivors. Many pairs of counter-balanced traits indicate excellent emotional intelligence. How do you compare? What contrary combinations would you add that describe you?

sensitive and tough

cautious and trusting

unselfish and selfish

serious and playful

self-appreciating and self-critical

sensible and irrational

creative and logical

impulsive and thorough

stable and unpredictable

hard-working and lazy

optimistic and pessimistic

Listen to Your Inner Voice
Something about adverse conditions opens people up to their intuitive abilities. Uncertainty and disorientation may make you more receptive to intuitive hunches about things than you normally would be. You may, for example, have a stronger sense of when you can or cannot trust what someone is saying.

Instead of dismissing these feelings, value them. You may
want to keep your awareness private, but monitor those
inner thoughts and feelings which come to you at this time.
They can serve to improve your sense of timing, and to
guide you through the maze of choices you face.

Practice Empathy
Resilient people have strong empathy skills. They have the
ability to see things from another person's point of view —
even someone they dislike. Ask yourself "What has the
downsizing and reorganization been like for the executives,
administrators, and managers?" "How do things look from
their perspective?"

Understanding how things look to someone who is threat-
ening your welfare may seem like a peculiar skill to develop, but asking yourself how the other person perceives
things may be the key that unlocks your next opportunity.

Don't misunderstand, however. Having empathy does not
mean you agree with a way of thinking you dislike. The
primary goal of empathy in a challenging situation is to
comprehend fully the thinking and needs of others so you
can develop an effective plan of action.

Develop empathy for everyone affected by the situation.
Ask yourself: "What do my co-workers feel and think?"
"How is my manager feeling?" "How do our clients and
customers see the situation?" "How is our competition
reacting?" "What does the public think?"

Empathy for others will make you more aware of what you
might do or say that will be useful and bring stability to the
turmoil. Empathy is a strong sign of emotional intelligence.

When an entire department was eliminated from a state agency, the scientists who were conducting federally-mandated testing were shocked. The work had to be done, or federal funding would be lost. Once they started problem-solving the situation, they saw that they were the best qualified people in the region to do the work. They formed a consulting firm, bid the job, and won the contract for doing the required work. An outcome they liked, because as consultants they paid themselves much more than they had earned as state employees.

Defend Yourself Well
People under pressure will say things about each other that are very insensitive. Resilient people don't let others abuse them emotionally. Practice having a few comments ready, such as: "I'm not interested in any gossip about me," or "I don't want to hear any negative comments right now." By being prepared for times when you hear criticisms, you will be unhurt by them when they arise, and you will avoid any mental drain they could place upon your resources. It may help to think of them as aftershocks, or flying shrapnel — dangerous and worth avoiding, but also something that happens during social earthquakes.

Help Others Cope
Researchers who study natural disasters find that a community's emergency workers (fire, police, medical, and service personnel) are less emotionally traumatized afterwards, even though they experience the same personal losses as others in their community. These findings suggest that if you are in a work group hit by a crisis, the best way to enhance your resiliency and avoid becoming mired in the group's victim feelings is to find ways to make yourself useful to others.

The point here is that it can be helpful both to others and to yourself to take time to ask your co-worker or your manager "How do you feel about what is happening?" and "Is there anything I can do to help?" Taking a few moments to let others know that you are concerned about them, usually has a very supportive effect.

Has downsizing or reorganization broken up your group of friendly co-workers? Write a letter of appreciation to the people you miss. List all the things you liked and appreciated about them. Your letter will help them boost their self-confidence any time they need it.

Become Synergistic
A synergistic person makes things work better for everyone. This is a very welcome person to have around. Striving to have things work well is almost always to your personal advantage. It is an example of enlightened selfishness. Don't hold back from assisting in a smooth transition just because you are angry and want to punish someone for what you feel has been done to you. Conduct yourself as a high-level professional, and be guided by your personal standards and values.

During times of crisis and change there are always a few solid people who are generous with their concern for others. Self-confident, mentally healthy people with professionalism are a source of reassurance and stability in chaotic situations. Such people stand out in the crowd. Be one of them.

Discover the Positive Side of Adversity
As was stated at the beginning, when you are hit by adversity you will never be the same again. Your struggle to bounce back and get your life back on track can develop strengths in you that you would not have gained otherwise. Friedrick Wilhelm Nietschze once said, "That which does not kill me makes me stronger." It isn't a way of gaining strength that people generally choose for themselves, but it is an inner capacity we all have.

Build Your Future With Highly Resilient People
To improve your chances of successes in your career and professional efforts, it is smart to surround yourself with people who are highly resilient. When you have choices about who you hire or associate with, interview them to see how closely they match up with the resiliency qualities listed in the quiz.

A woman who was building her CPA practice knew that many people who own small businesses get into financial difficulty. She decided to only accept clients who matched the descriptions of highly resilient survivors. When approached by potential clients she would take them to lunch, saying she wanted to get to know them first. She would ask many questions about various challenges they had encountered and asked how things turned out. She says she only accepted about one out of three as clients and by doing so built a very successful practice because her clients rarely went bankrupt. It was just the opposite. They kept growing their businesses and hers grew as well.

When you master all four levels of resiliency, you can cope and even thrive in rough situations that overwhelm others. And beyond that, because of your synergistic nature, you have energy for helping other people get through rough times as well.

An Excellent Sign of Wisdom: TheTalent for Serendipity

Is wisdom something you have, or something you use? My view is that wisdom is a unique a combination of many qualities that leads to a person being highly life-competent.

Tom Peterson worked for many years to build a strong business selling television sets, stereo systems, and home appliances. He gave people good value, a full satisfaction guarantee, and friendly service. With the help of his wife Gloria, who handled the books, Tom developed an excellent reputation. He was proud of his high percentage of repeat customers.

Tom advertised heavily on television and in newspapers. He became known for his trademark crew cut and his cheery, early morning television commercials. If you saw the movie "Raising Arizona," you saw Tom Peterson's commercial played in the early morning motel room scene.

In 1990, Tom was approached by the owners of a competing company, Stereo Super Stores. They wanted him to buy them out. The price was very attractive. He examined their books, looked at their inventory, talked to employees, sized up the store locations, and looked at the leases. Everything looked good. Here was a chance to eliminate a competitor and expand his business. His bankers said they would loan him whatever he needed to make the purchase.

Before making his final decision, Tom asked Gloria what she thought about the purchase. She told him that even though the numbers looked good it didn't feel right to her. He asked her to explain why, but she couldn't. She told him she had a strong feeling that he shouldn't purchase the Stereo Super Stores.

Tom was so self-confident, however, and so convinced that this was a rare opportunity, he went ahead and made the purchase. Within months he discovered that he had made a big mistake. He had paid much too much for a dying company. He tried as hard as he could to make it work out, but he couldn't turn things around. Three years later, he was close to bankruptcy. He was about to lose everything, including his original business.

A survey had identified Tom as the best-known business-man in Oregon. When highly visible people make mistakes, their mistakes are highly visible. Tom was embarrassed, but he is a resilient survivor. He looked at his situation. He decided to admit his mistake openly and, rather than getting bogged down in lawsuits, he focused his energies on saving and rebuilding his original business. He saw also that he had made a mistake by not listening to his wife, and that he needed to learn from this experience. He made a new television commercial that started with him saying:

> *"I should have listened to my wife! When Gloria told me not to buy the Stereo 'Stupid' Stores, I should have listened to her. I made a mistake, but we're still in business — with a new name. We are now Tom Peterson and Gloria's too. We have some great bargains for you at the old store this weekend..."*

Tom played up his mistake in judgment. He dealt with the crisis in a way that endeared him to many people and increased their respect for him. Old customers flocked into his store. To survive financially, Tom had to close a warehouse and lay off employees. He began to use supply system management that he had never attempted before. He advertised products in newspaper and television ads while the trucks from the manufacturers were on the way to his store.

> *"In the years before my struggle to survive,"* Tom
> *says with a big grin, "I was turning inventory three*
> *times a year. Now I'm turning inventory twelve times*
> *a year with fewer employees and higher profit margins."*

Difficulties bring gifts to the people who look for them. Tom not only fought back from the edge of financial disaster to build a better business than before, he has discovered an additional "gift" from the experience. When business groups and professional associations asked Tom to speak to them about how he was able to handle his business crisis so successfully, Tom saw the opportunity. He now gives motivational and entertaining talks to many business groups on "How I Became a Millionaire Twice!"

The Talent for Serendipity
People with wisdom have a knack for finding a hidden gift in misfortune. They have a talent for serendipity. The statement "It was the best thing that every happened to me" is a primary indicator that someone has learned how to be highly resilient and life-competent.

Have you found a gift in an accident or misfortune? Take a few moments to reflect on a difficult past experience and describe something beneficial that you had the wisdom to find in it.

The term "serendipity" was created by the English writer
Horace Walpole. It was a talent he recognized in himself,
but when he tried to write to a friend about it, there were no
good words to describe the ability. He coined the term from
his memory of a Persian children's tale about the "Three
Princes From the Land of Serendip." Walpole insisted that
serendipity was not "good luck." He said that there had to be:

(1)   an accident or potential misfortune
(2)   that a person had the good sense or wisdom to
(3)   convert into a beneficial outcome.

By looking for the positive aspects in potential misfortune
you will be able to welcome the events taking place and be
thankful for them. This reaction is a powerful way to avoid
feeling like a helpless victim. When you are going through a
transition you may not have wanted and don't like, there
will be things you do like about it, and things which may
turn out to be to your advantage.

An interesting thing about the human brain is that when
you send it looking for information, it often finds it. If you
define the situation too narrowly and think of it only as
ruining your life, then information which seems contrary to
your mind-set, such as possible good fortune or opportunity, won't be able to penetrate your perspective. People
who turn "misfortune" into opportunity do so because they
deliberately scan for those opportunities. It is a powerful
skill which life's best survivors share. It is called the serendipity talent.

Lance Armstrong, famous for winning many Tour deFrance bicycle races, says "If I had to choose between getting testicular cancer and winning the Tour de France, I would choose testicular cancer." He describes his bout with cancer as "a special wake-up call." He says the cancer left him scarred physically and emotionally, but says "it was an unexpected gift." He says his recovery ordeal changed him. It made him fully appreciate the blessings of good health, a loving family, and close friends.

The talent for serendipity is having the wisdom to discover good fortune in situations that appear to be tragic. People like Lance Armstrong, who create success out of apparent disaster, do not merely rise above their problems, they discover good fortune in misfortune.

You were born with the ability to learn how to gain strength from life's trials. What you are going through could be one of the best things that ever happened to you. When disruptive changes never seem to stop, highly resilient people find ways to sustain themselves and avoid resiliency fatigue — even when events are unwanted and feel unfair. The best long-term strategy is to handle each disruption as well as you can, adapt quickly, and choose to make the effort to bounce back. It isn't pleasant at the time, but your effort can lead to becoming increasingly resilient, more self-confident, stronger, and better.

Review

Take time to reflect on what these chapters on resiliency have meant to you. What information has been most useful? What new abilities have you gained? To help in your review, rate yourself from 1-5 on the following:

☐ I maintain my health, energy, and emotional stability by expressing feelings and doing what revitalizes me.

☐ I respond to difficulties in active, effective ways.

☐ I avoid feeling bitter about unfair events and don't feel like a victim.

☐ I respond to adversity using good problem-solving.

☐ My self-confidence, self-esteem, and self-concept are healthy and strong.

☐ I have a strong attitude of professionalism, can work effectively without a job description.

☐ I received high scores on the quiz items in "How Resilient Are You?"

☐ I enjoy and value my paradoxical nature. I'm able to be both optimistic and pessimistic about reaching my goals.

☐ I'm good at learning lessons in the school of life.

☐ I'm known for being able to make things work well.

☐ Some of my worst experiences in life have been very good for me.

Note: If you have a personal resiliency story that you are willing to share about successful problem-solving or overcoming adversity, please let Al Siebert know at the Resiliency Center web site:

www.resiliencycenter.com

Sharing
The Flame

Gail Tycer, M.S.

What You Need to Know About Writing to Communicate

Remember the last time you read an unclear letter, memo, or e-mail that left you wondering what the writer meant, or what you were supposed to do about it? Did you feel it was your responsibility to figure out what he or she was trying to tell you? Or was it more likely — I know you're a kind person, but be painfully honest here — was it more likely that you felt the writer probably didn't know what he or she was talking about?

That's how our readers feel about us. If they don't get it at a glance, they decide we don't know what we are talking about.

All the information and knowledge you and I have worked so hard over the years to gain will come to nothing if we cannot communicate it to others. How you write — how you communicate in writing — could be the single most important business success skill you possess.

You and I are judged — and can only judge others — by what they know of us, or by what we know of them. It may or may not be entirely fair, but the truth is that if all they know of us is what we have written, then that's exactly how we, or our company, will be judged. By our writing.

Clear writing, strategic writing, builds credibility and reinforces professionalism. To get ahead on the job, or in our
own businesses, we must develop the skills professional
writers use to write less, say more—and get results! It starts
with what I call

The Process.
Step 1: Writing starts with an idea. You may have an idea
for something you might communicate, or someone else
gives you one. Do a quick reality check. Does this information need to be passed along—at all? Many of the people
I've worked with in my seminars and coaching over the
years have told me that this one step has cut their writing
time by as much as 50%!

Step 2: For the moment, let's assume that this idea, this
information, should be passed along. If so, should it be
passed along in writing—including e-mail, of course? Or
communicated in some other way?

Why write? You may think of others, but let's consider a
few of the main reasons for writing, instead of picking up
the phone, stopping by someone's desk, or putting the
information on the grapevine.

Perhaps the most significant strategic reason for writing is
to give a weight to a message that the spoken word simply
does not give. How many times have we heard variations
on, *"They wouldn't write it down if it weren't true!"* That's the
weight I'm talking about.

But also, we write to document; to provide a reference; when there is a specific mandate to do so (personnel matters, for one example); and when we need to get the same message to a number of readers at the same time.

Step 3: The next step is to develop our focus, and the strategy for the piece. I recommend my Strategic Business Writing Blueprint for this process. Here's where you get focused. Here's where you determine your results. Focus allows you to get started quickly, easily. Focus is the best thing I know to avoid writers' block. Focus also gives you content.

Step 4: Get started right. Carefully craft that first sentence or two. Make sure your reader will get it at a glance.

Step 5: Gather and organize your content. Edit before you write. Tighten it up, and look for alternate formats to make your meaning clear. Finish strong.

Step 6: Run a final quick check to make sure you've done what you intended to do.

Now, let's spend the balance of this chapter on the Strategic Business Writing Blueprint.

When I developed the Strategic Business Writing Blueprint some years ago, I thought of it as a pre-writing discipline to help writers get started. Surprisingly, the feedback I've gotten over the years is that it is also a good way to avoid what I call the *bounceback syndrome* — you know, where you are given a piece to write, you write it, and then you get it back for rewrite, and back, and back. When you and the person who has asked you to write the piece can agree before you start to write, you have objective criteria to measure against. His or her review no longer consists of his or her "I think" vs. your "I think." (We all know who wins that argument!)

First, consider the overall strategy of your piece — what I've called **The Purpose Statement**. Here's what you need to do:

(1) Identify the piece specifically. This means that you say, "I am going to write a one-paragraph memo," or "I am going to write a one-screen e-mail."

See the completed piece in your mind's eye before you begin to write it. If this seems excessive, or even a bit strange, do me a favor, and just try it. Identifying the piece specifically helps you to determine automatically which content to include, and what you can leave out. When we're talking "quick and easy," this is a good starting point!

(2) Identify the reader by name. This automatically calls up your mental "data base" on this person, and helps you to consider the approach that might be the most effective.

(3) Identify your purpose for writing. This is the most critical step of all. Even if you do everything else right, if you miss this step, there are no guarantees your writing will work the way you want it to.

Let me digress here for a moment, and ask you, "What is writing?" Please pause for just a moment, and consider this question carefully.

What is writing? I've had a lot of answers to this question: "a way of communicating," "a way to express yourself," "a way to make things clear," and so on. What was your answer? The fact is, each of these answers is at least partially correct — but partially incorrect as well. Writing may or may not do these things for you, and in any case, may or may not be your only choice for doing them.

As a professional writer — unlike the English teachers who may have assured us that if we just used correct grammar and punctuation, and spelled correctly, all would be well — I prefer to consider writing not as an end to itself, but as a tool. A tool to get a job done.

From this perspective, it only makes sense that we determine what that job is before we start to write.

End of digression. Back to the point. Why are you writing?

What is your purpose for writing? In my experience, there are two reasons for writing: (1) to inform; or (2) to persuade. If you find any others, please let me know.

If you are writing to inform, you will use words like "inform," "tell," "state," or "notify." And in terms of results, the reader is on his or her own. You don't care. You are presenting the information objectively, and whatever the reader decides to do with, or about the information you are providing, is up to him or her.

If you are writing to persuade, you will use words like "persuade," "motivate," "convince," or "justify." Of course you will present information — generally information selected to build your point. But unlike writing purely on the informa-

tion side, when you are writing to persuade, you do care
what happens, and you will carefully plan for results.

(4) Identify your content in general terms. Take a look at
(a) the specific piece you are writing, (b) the reader by
name, (c) your purpose for writing (inform or persuade),
and (d) considering the first three steps, what is it you want
to say?

Your purpose statement (on the information side) will now
sound something like this: "I am going to write a one-paragraph memo to Joe Jones, informing him of the ABC Committee meeting at 2 p.m. Friday in Conference Room A."

Note how different that is from this purpose statement, on
the persuasion side: "I am going to write a one-paragraph
memo to Joe Jones, persuading him to attend the ABC Committee meeting at 2 p.m. Friday in Conference Room A."

Next, plan for results. Use the two most useful words in
the English language, "so that." For example, "I am going
to write a one-paragraph memo to Joe Jones, persuading
him to attend the ABC Committee meeting at 2 p.m. Friday
in Conference Room A, *so that* (a) he will know when and
where the meeting is; (b) he will understand why he needs
to attend; (c) he will come; (d) he will be prepared.

Then, decide on the tone you will use. Tone is the relationship the writer sets up with the reader. Everyone will use
different words. How would you describe the relationship
you want with your reader? "Professional?" "Objective?"
"Friendly?" "Knowledgeable?" "Helpful?" "Authoritative?"

Finally, list the items you want to discuss; the points you want to make. Ask yourself, "Why does my reader need this information?" "How will he or she use it?" and then, "What is my purpose for writing?" Now make a list. Use just a few words to remind yourself what you want to talk about.

Now you have your Strategic Business Writing Blueprint: (1) The purpose statement; (2) Planned Results ("so that's"), (3) Tone (the relationship you set up with your reader); and (4) Content (based on your reader's need and use for this information, and on your purpose for writing). Now you're ready to write that first paragraph.

How to Start Writing
Quickly and Easily
...and Cut a Page or Two Down to 3-5 Lines,
So Your Reader "Gets It" at a Glance,
and Admires Your Professional
Knowledge and Credibility

If I could give you one skill; show you one trick that would transform your writing overnight—would you be interested?

Then read on, because this chapter will show you how to write the first paragraph of your e-mail, memo, or letter. How to turn that one page to page-and-a-half letter into a single paragraph, three to five lines.

You'll learn how to make your point quickly; how to establish your professionalism and reinforce your credibility. You'll soon be able to take advantage of your reader's fleeting 100% attention level. And you'll develop a technique to prepare your reader to accept your message.

It all happens with the "lead" sentence or paragraph. How you construct this first three to five lines will be critical to how your reader receives your message, and what he or she will think of you and of your company.

To begin with, regardless of what our third grade teachers may have told us about paying better attention, the real-life fact of the matter is that human beings are not built to pay 100% attention 100% of the time. We can't do it! It's just not how we were made. And if we can't do it, it's a cinch our reader cannot do it either.

What the first paragraph looks like is critical. How your reader "gets it" (or not) is very much a function of how those words look on paper, or in an e-mail attached file.

Why three to five lines — and no more? Research shows that the average adult reader's 100% attention span will diminish somewhere between lines three and five. You can push it to line five if that's the end of the paragraph, and the double space between paragraphs is there to offer the eye some relief.

Take a look at the following two examples:

Which would you rather read? Which do you think your
reader would rather read?

The first paragraph of the sample on the right takes advantage
of your reader's natural 100% attention span. Here's where his
or her 100% attention is most likely to be. After that, attention
tends to diminish — perhaps to 10% here; 90% there, and everywhere in between. Obviously it's to your advantage to get
your message into the first paragraph, which will be no more
than three to five lines. Three to five lines will probably be one
or two sentences, three at the very most.

Now what happens in the sample on the left? You're building
a fence to keep the reader out, simply by how it looks — and
not a gate, such as the first paragraph of the right-hand
sample.

If you want your reader to "get it" at a glance, this first paragraph will do it for you, if you structure it to contain certain
information. You've heard this probably a hundred times
before, but it is absolutely critical that this information be
included in the first paragraph. Here's the formula: Who +
What + When + Where + Why + How = Clarity.

Although most sentences start with the "who" doing the
"what," these elements may be in any order in your lead
sentence. "Why" is the strongest element, both for building
your persuasive case, and for establishing relevance (your
reader wants to know "why should I read this?") when you're
writing on the information side.

Experiment. When you're writing to persuade, you'll probably want to start your lead sentence or paragraph with the "why," say, seven out of ten times. Here's an example:

Sentence 1: I will need your completed time sheets hand-carried to my office no later than 5:00 p.m. on the 27th of each month so you can continue to receive your paycheck on time.

Sentence 2: So you can continue to receive your paycheck on time, I will need your completed time sheets hand-carried to my office no later than 5:00 p.m. on the 27th of each month.

Do you see the difference? Exactly the same words, placed in a different order in the sentence. Which is more persuasive? Have a bit of fun with your writing! Move the various elements around, and see what different effects you can achieve.

Remember: A "lead" paragraph—that first paragraph of three to five lines and one or two, and at the most three sentences, containing who, (did) what, when, where, why, and how—is a special type of sentence. It will be different from virtually every other sentence in the piece.

In addition to how it looks, your lead paragraph or sentence must be (1) complete (who + what + when + where + why + how); (2) concise (no extra words or phrases—no "freeloaders"—every word or phrase must have a job); and (3) must also pass the five-year test.

Taking these one at a time, (1) we already know "complete" means each of the six w-w-w-w-w-h elements is in the sentence; by (2) "concise," we mean that all the deadwood—all

the extra words—has been removed. Take the following
sentence for example:

> Your attorney requested that we forward the en-
> closed materials to you direct from our office today
> via air express, so you could use them in preparing
> your testimony for the Senate subcommittee.

Let's analyze this sentence for completeness:

(Your attorney) **Who**

(requested that we forward the enclosed materials) **What**

(to you) **Where**

direct from our office

(today) **When**

(via air express,) **How**

(so you could use them in preparing your testimony for the
Senate subcommittee.) **Why**

So, as we see, the sentence is complete. But is it concise?
Where are the "freeloader words"? Right. "direct from our
office"does not have a job. Delete that phrase!

The sentence now reads:

> Your attorney requested that we forward the en-
> closed materials to you today via air express, so you
> could use them in preparing your testimony for the
> Senate subcommittee.

Perhaps not the best sentence in the world, but certainly an improvement over version one, and it makes our point. So now our sentence is complete, and concise. Does it pass the five-year test?

Pretend that five years from now someone picks your memo, or e-mail printout from the file. Will that person, who was not involved, know what you're talking about? What will his or her questions be? (Take a minute to think about this before going on to the next paragraph.)

In the exercise sentence, we will assume that the date is at the top of the piece, so "today" would be clear. Perhaps the reader would want to know the name of the attorney? Or the nature of the enclosed materials? Or the name of the air express carrier? Or which senate subcommittee? Or the hearing date? Here's one way we might pass the five-year test:

> Your attorney, Joe Jones, requested that we for-ward the enclosed budget materials to you today via FedEx, so you could use them in preparing your October 3 testimony for the Senate Finance Subcommittee.

Or, in two shorter sentences:

> Your attorney, Joe Jones, requested that we forward the enclosed budget materials to you via FedEx today. He thought they could be of value to you in preparing your October 3 testimony for the Senate Finance Subcommittee.

To make sure you know who's who, and what's what, practice a bit on the following sentences. Remember "Who" does, or will do, or has done, "What." The "What" is the action of the "Who." "Who" does "What."

Your assignment: (1) Check each of the following sentences for completeness. (2) Go back and add any elements missing from each sentence. (3) Go back to each sentence and chop out any freeloading words or phrases. (4) Do a final check to add any "five-year test" content needed. (5) Go back for the last time, and, being careful not to eliminate any of the "complete" or "five-year test" elements, do a final edit on each sentence.

A. I have contacted Joe Jones of Jones Company in regard to our office requirements.

( ) who ( ) what ( ) when ( ) where ( ) why ( ) how

B. The company requires certain information from each department concerning its projected needs, and will appreciate your participation.

( ) who ( ) what ( ) when ( ) where ( ) why ( ) how

C. Please send your check so we may reinstate your coverage.

( ) who ( ) what ( ) when ( ) where ( ) why ( ) how

Sentence A, you will notice, has a who (I), and a what (have contacted). It has no when or how, so you will need to add these two elements. The where and the why are weak, at best. The partial where (of Jones Company) could be clarified by adding "Chicago," for instance, if there is more than one Jones Company location. The incomplete why (in regard to our office requirements) sounds pretty good at first glance. Then think about it. Could someone realistically be expected to work from this information? Probably not. Office requirements for what? Software? Personnel? File cabinets? Petty Cash?

Sentence B has a who (The company) and a what (requires). But what are the company's chances of getting the information it requires if it does not tell the reader when it's needed; where to send it; why it's needed; or how to send it? Slim to none, would you say? To make Sentence B into a complete lead sentence or paragraph, add the when, where, why, and how.

Sentence C likewise has some tricks to it. The who in this case is "you, understood." This is a convention in our English language that says when a sentence starts with an action word — as so many instructions and documentations do — we "understand" that a "You" could be put in front of the action word. For example, (You) please send your check....

So there is a who ("You"), a what (please send your check), and a why (so we may reinstate your coverage). We need to add the when, the where, and the how to send it, to make this a complete lead sentence.

But wait! There's more. Probably the most useful question to
ask yourself when you are trying to motivate action, is "What
comes next?" In this case, our reader rushes home to find that
he or she is without insurance, and must send a check to
reinstate coverage. You're ahead of me now, right? If you ask
yourself "What comes next?" the big question becomes, for
what amount should the check be written?

Always ask yourself "What comes next for the reader to do
what I'm asking him or her to do?"

Now, the moment you've been waiting for: You are going to
write your own lead paragraph. (1) Starting with the Strategic
Business Writing Blueprint from the preceding chapter, identify, and develop a strategy for a piece you have to write. Be
sure it is a "real" piece.

(2) Next, write the first sentence. Go ahead, just write it. Write
it quickly. Write the first thing you can think of that needs to
be said. Don't try to make it perfect, or worry about how good
it is. Then go back and review it, just as we did above. Make
sure it is complete, concise, and would pass the five-year test.
If not, touch it up where needed—just as we did above. When
you're happy with it, ask yourself "What comes next." Touch
it up, tighten and polish it—and that's all there is to it!

You have made your point so the reader can "get it" at a
glance.

You are the proud author of three to five lines that will — at least 50% of the time, I'm convinced — replace the cumbersome page to page-and-a-half you used to write. You have made your point quickly, which establishes your professionalism and reinforces your credibility. You've reached your reader where he or she is most likely to be paying 100% attention. And if your message could not be completed in that three to five lines, your reader is prepared for what follows. Good job!

17 Ways to Increase Your Comfort Level, Enhance Your Professionalism, & Generally Feel Better About Your Presentation

Throughout your business and personal life, there will always be opportunities to present your thoughts, ideas, needs to appropriate audiences. If you can speak well, you possess that rare skill that can enhance not only your own personal and business life and career, but can do great things for communities and people whose causes you may enthusiastically champion.

And yet, most people would rather face a root canal without anesthetic than stand up in front of even a few people to speak.

Here are 17 things to think about as you prepare for your next presentation:

Before the presentation,

1. Test Your Title. If you can comfortably do so, call several individuals who will be in your audience. Give them a choice of three titles; ask which one they like the best — or perhaps they have another title in mind? Then ask them, "If you were to listen to a presentation titled (the name they chose) what would you expect to learn?" This gives you both a great title, and the content your audience wants to hear.

2. Make the Room Yours. When you can, go to the room where your presentation will be held, while it is still empty. Stand in the front of the room. In the back. At the sides. Visualize your audience as though they were there. "Feel" the room; make it feel as comfortable to you as your own home. Then it will be easy to welcome your audience into "your space," just as you would if you were welcoming them into your home.

3. Work the Room. Now the audience is beginning to enter. A trickle at first, then more, and more. Greet newcomers as they come in. Walk over to those already seated, if you missed them at the door. Introduce yourself. Ask them questions about their businesses, or about their lives, to give you a sense of what they are there to hear. This allows you to refer to several of them by name, and, with their permission, to refer briefly to several of these conversations during your presentation. As you can thus tailor your comments to the needs of your audience, they will appreciate them (and you!) much more.

During the presentation,

4. Be Prepared. This is the key to dry palms. If you know what you want to say, what you want to say about it, and how you're going to say it, you're halfway there.

5. Don't Sweat the Small Stuff (Or the Big Stuff, Either!) When I was a child at my mother's knee, she told me, "You wouldn't worry so much about what people think of you if you realized how seldom they do!" Sage words, indeed. Many would-be speakers are so focused on what their audiences will think about them, that they forget they are there to focus on the audience, and its needs.

Concentrate on what unique information you have that your audience wants to, craves to, needs to hear. Focus on meeting their needs with your presentation. Do that, and I guarantee your success!

6. Your Audience Wants You to Succeed. Ben Padrow, perhaps one of the best speech coaches ever, liked to remind his students that, "Your audience does not want to be bored. They will do everything in their power to help you succeed!" Your audience is your best ally. They are fully on your side.

7. Get Close to the Audience. Most of your presentations are likely to be to groups of fewer than 100. If you can be seen and heard, be "on the floor" with your audience. Walk up to them individually. Whether or not you can be physically with them, you can still connect with them. Anchor your points. Briefly look each individual in the eye. Pause to let your points sink in. Focus on faces in the audience, rather than looking somewhere over their heads.

8. Use Visuals for Notes. Overheads. Posters. Slides. The same handout materials they have in front of them. This will keep you on track, and, as you are speaking "without notes," help you to present your message, and yourself, as a knowledgeable professional.

A word about PowerPoint presentations: Do not read the screeens to your audience. They can do that for themselves. Instead, provide additional information on your points that relates to, but is not on the screen. And by all means, keep the audience lights on! Just dim the lights so the screen can be read easily.

9. Be Sensitive to Gender References. It used to be, and still is, in some academic settings, that the pronoun "he" was a one-size-fits-all. No more! Be careful to use "he or she"when the gender is uncertain or undefined. Not only is it far more accurate and appropriate, but this usage should not offend your audience, and will avoid making you look old-fashioned, or dated.

10. Use the Full Vocal Range. We all know that monotone is deadly. To keep your audience awake, vary the volume, pitch, and pace of your comments. Loud sometimes, normal, even a whisper if it can be heard. Each is effective in itself, but especially so when you vary the volume throughout. Tone of voice and pitch — high, low, medium — is effective for emphasizing your points. And remember the strategic pause!

11. Your Body Language Speaks as Loudly as Your Words. Stand tall, shoulders back, to build your credibility. This makes you look like you know what you're talking about, and believe what you're saying. Keep in mind the difference between a drooping-shoulders slouch, and a purposeful lean toward your audience when you have confidential, or "inside" information to impart. A slouch just makes you look tired and unsure. Match your body language to your content.

12. Stay Upbeat! With a possible few exceptions — I can't think of any at the moment — your audience wants a positive, upbeat presentation style. Enthusiasm is a good thing.

13. They're Not Mad, Just Concentrating. Most of us are, consciously or unconsciously, sensitive to audience body language. At some point you may even have taken a course, or heard a lecture on the subject. Keep in mind that what we have learned may be good guidelines, but not infallible. One person's angry face may be another's way of concentrating.

14. They May be Mad, But Not at You. Of course they may be, but until you're sure that (a) they are mad; and (b) they're mad at you, assume they are not. More likely, something outside of the presentation room is with them mentally — a work or family issue, a tough decision — the sort of thing that has little or nothing to do with you, or with your presentation.

15. Walk Toward a Disagreeing or Heckling Audience Member. But not if you feel this would put you in harm's way. Often a specific audience member may be giving you a hard time because he or she feels the need for attention, which again actually has little or nothing to do with you or with your presentation. Others, of course, may have their own agendas; take a political meeting, or public hearing for example. It's harder to disagree or heckle effectively when the speaker is next to you.

16. Let Your Audience Develop Your Talk for You. This will not do away with the need for preparation — if anything, you may have to be more prepared when you're not sure what the questions will be. From time to time when appropriate, ask your audience what they specifically want to know. Then tell them.

And finally,

17. Tell Them What They Learned (and How to Use It, in Terms of Benefits to Them). The same teacher was, every year, year after year after year, named the top public school teacher in her district. One day I asked her how she did it. Her reply? "What is the first question a parent asks his or her child when that child comes home from school? I want to be sure each of my students has a good answer, so for a few minutes before they leave for the day, I review with them what we did, and what they learned!"

What You Need to Understand About Marketing to Build Your Career or Your Business

Fact: The market drives acceptance or rejection of your product. Whether they buy or don't buy determines whether the company will thrive, do well, stagger along, or die. And ultimately, how well you will do.

If you are an employee, building your career, this chapter is for you. If you are further along in your career, then this chapter is for you. And if you are wondering why you have not done better with your career, then this chapter is for you.

And especially if you have made that leap of faith, and have started your own business, this chapter is definitely for you.

The old attitude of "If I just do my job, that's all I need to do, and all I need to know," is a dead-end street. You've got to understand the basic components of marketing to be a partner in building your company, and to develop a strong sales message. That's where your real value comes in: You are most valuable when you can help build the business by applying a marketing orientation to your unique expertise, in your unique area. That's how careers, and lives, are built to prosper.

Take these basics, and use them as building blocks. These are your guidelines for where to look, and what questions to ask. Once you understand, and apply them to your business, you will be able to make career-building recommendations; to position yourself within your organization; or to build your own thriving business.

The term"marketing" is vague in many business people's minds. Many have the idea that marketing = sales. Or, alternatively, that marketing = advertising and promotion.

Each is true to a degree. For now, let's define marketing as "every consideration necessary to sell your product, service, cause, candidate, or idea to those who have the need or desire, and the resources to do what you're asking them to do."

I like to start the process by thinking of three interlocking circles — each a subsystem of the overall marketing system:

(1) Product (Service)/Pricing /Packaging;
(2) Distribution; and
(3) Communication.

The successful business will operate in the area where all three are working together.

Let's look at them one at a time.

Product (Service)/Pricing/Packaging
Product/Service
If you're selling a service, think of it as a product. The first key in successfully marketing your product (or service) may seem obvious: Is it a good one? Will it do the job the buyer expects it to do? Who will buy it at the price you must charge to meet your objectives?

Here is the critical issue: Assuming you have assured yourself you have a good product, fairly priced, are there enough prospective buyers who are both willing and able to pay the price you must charge? The answer to this consideration will not only drive your product (or service) development, but your pricing strategy as well.

Now that you know who will buy at your price, ask yourself: "Why do they buy mine? Why do they use mine?" (Think about it — these are two very different questions — and could determine who your best prospects will be. They could be the ones buying, but not the ones using your product or service.)

How will they/do they use it? Why do they prefer it to others? Will they buy it regularly, or one time? Why? Will they recommend it to their friends? How can you build repeat business? Referral business? Where is new business likely to come from?

And then: Who, exactly, is your competition? (The answer to this question may be surprising!) How do you compare? What is the competition likely to do next? And for that matter, what do you intend to do next! (Remember that two of the most critical words in the marketing lexicon are "so that.")

Pricing
Do your product homework thoroughly. If your pricing is high, is there a way to reduce the cost of manufacture? To re-position your product for higher perceived value? Can you either "bundle," or "unbundle" your product or service to reach an acceptable price?

Could you take a portion (most definitely not all) of your price in some sort of a trade for your customer's goods or services? Could you apportion the cost of your product or service so it could be charged to various of your customer's budget accounts, rather than coming out of just one?

If your pricing is too low, consider raising it. Pricing can have a significant impact on perceived value — and relates directly to your target prospect. You may develop a more profitable business by selling less of your service or product, at a higher price.

Could you be asking so little for your product or service that you are positioning it as somehow second rate? On the other hand, is "bargain days" the position that will work best for you? This position has made millionaires, too!

Packaging
Packaging — whether for a service, or for a product — must be consistent with your pricing and image, as well as with the place where it will be sold, or made available. When your product's packaging does not reflect your image, or your product personality, you are sending mixed messages. That is asking for trouble.

For a service business, packaging could include how you present yourself — your overall "presence" — dress, grooming, how you talk, and generally how you present yourself, your company, and your product or service. It could also include your location, if customers come to you.

Everything does not have to be done, or presented, in the most costly way. "Capable," "professional," or "competent" do not necessarily mean you must drive a new car or dress expensively. Think about your clients and prospects, and present yourself appropriately to meet their expectations, while remaining consistent with your image.

You have a good product or service, fairly priced to give you the return you must have. There are enough prospective buyers who are both willing and able to pay your price, and you have a good understanding of their decision-making process and buying habits. And you know the competition.

Next, we'll look at marketing's other two subsystems, Distribution, and Communication:

Distribution

Consider how (and where) your customer gets your product or service. What kind of a business are you? Should you be? Wholesale? Retail? Service? MLM? Do you sell on the internet? Do you sell only on the internet, or do you use supplementary sales channels? Do you sell by mail order? Make in-person sales calls, take orders over the telephone?

Do you use independent wholesalers, distributors, sales representatives? Do you sell through your own store, office, or facility? Through others' locations? What criteria have you established for those locations?

How do you deliver your product or service to your customer? And just who is your customer, anyway? If you sell through retail stores, for example, the store owner, or buyer, or purchasing decision-maker, will be your customer. Understanding who your customer really is can increase your sales significantly, and will, obviously, have a strong impact on your product line.

If you purchase raw or manufactured materials or products, consider your shipping costs. They could have significant input into your product line and pricing. If costs push you to a level where you cannot make an appropriate return by selling

at a competitive price, look for new ways to ship or to manufacture. Or raise the price.

Communication
Here's where you consider advertising, promotion, publicity,
trade shows, public relations — even structured word-of-
mouth. In short, any planned activity that gets the good word
out for you.

The keys to successful communication:

> (1) Understand your target audience;
> (2) Know your competition, and your significant points
>   of difference; and
> (3) Frame your message in terms of benefits to your
>   target audience.

Should you advertise? "Advertising" refers to paid media
advertising, which is purchased on the basis of Reach and
Frequency — how often can you reach how many — and at
what cost.

Many small businesses, and, increasingly, mid-size to large
businesses are realizing that there are ways to build a business
that money can't buy. Brains can substitute for dollars. And
frequently have to.

Profitable sales are the result of successful marketing activity.
Advertising and promotion are only two of the vehicles that
may advance your company.   When advertising is needed,
nothing will substitute. Yet frequently I counsel my clients in
other, more cost-effective directions.

Although there are exceptions, advertising in mass media most often works best for large companies who have
    (1) a broad target audience, and
    (2) the resources to pay for lots of messages, often.

Because many businesses have tightly-targeted audiences, and limited resources, media advertising is not always the most cost-effective — or even the best — solution. The challenge is to reach the largest number of qualified prospects at the right time, and at the lowest cost. You might consider:

For print advertising: Try listings in well-used, targeted directories; neighborhood papers; trade publications if you sell within a certain industry, or to a certain profession; classified ads in major papers if you have a consumer product or service, or one that fits into a well-read category; or perhaps "shoppers."

Direct mail is most likely a better bet for you. You can control the budget; the medium is highly flexible and can be tightly targeted; and results are easily measurable.

Or consider directing an e-mail campaign to prospects who have indicated an interest in hearing from you.

For radio and television advertising: Consider off-hours or bargain packages only on stations targeted to your prospects and customers if, and only if, that's when they will be listening.

For outdoor advertising: A single outdoor board could work to direct traffic to your retail operation, but weigh carefully the results against the cost.

For Yellow Pages: What does your competition do? Frequently, your listing will be enough.

If you do decide to advertise, look for opportunities to share costs with non-competitive advertisers; and take advantage of co-op opportunities offered by your suppliers.

Promotion, publicity, trade shows, public relations — even structured word-of-mouth; referrals, repeat business, and additional business from the same customer will be your best bets for building your business. And remember, if there's a chance your customers and prospects will be looking for your web site online — be there.

Fanning
The Flame

Jerry Fletcher
The Networking Ninja

Crowd of One

One ability marks the difference between start-up companies that fly and those that die.

One skill marks the boundary between success and failure.

One gift can turn your life from loneliness to joy.

Whether you bootstrap it, find a mentor, or simply get lucky there is a single restraint.

One.

One look in a mirror can show you who controls your fate.

How good are you at building relationships? Can you convince someone to believe in your vision? Are you sure you can convince that special someone to consider a life with you?

Building a business, a career, or finding the love of your life are all about your ability to connect with people — Networking. Businesses, careers, and lives of joy are all built one connection at a time — one connection plus another and another until you have a crowd.

That crowd starts with an individual and a commitment.

The fortune cookie version of building your crowd reads like this:

> The wise man knows his limits…
> A shrewd one his resources…
> Ultimately it's not who you know that matters
> As much as who you trust (and who trusts you).

Here's how to put that "pearl of wisdom" to work for you:

1. **A wise man or woman knows his or her limits.** You can't do everything well. One, yes, even two or three things, but not everything. No one can. And no one expects you to.

   Hone your skills. What you can do is just as important as who you know. Demonstrate your abilities to a broadening circle of people who can refer you and your career will move at a faster pace. Adding the power of their network to yours multiplies your possibilities.

   Going into business? It takes a multitude of talents to build and run a profitable company. Gather to you all the talent and skills that your company needs to survive and thrive. Build those relationships. Work at being sure that all of those people see your vision and are actively pursuing it with you. Ask them to share that vision with the people who are their resources. Over time you want their network to be intimately connected to yours.

   Finding Mr. or Ms. Right is part of the same equation. Don't try to be what you aren't. And don't expect him or her to be, either. Be candid and you'll discover if you might like to know each other for a long time — if only as friends.

2. **A shrewd man or woman knows his or her resources.** To succeed, gather a group of successful resources., Model the behavior of successful people.

    Most importantly, especially in the early phases, make sure you judge people by what they do, rather than by what they say. Some will tell you virtually anything you want to hear, but when you look at what they've accomplished the ledger is blank. Successful people and professionals don't operate that way.

    Professionals get that designation by having a talent, developing it, and practicing their skills until they can deliver predictable results. That makes them successful.

    Look for successful people. They move. They act. They get things done. They make a measurable difference.

    Model them.

    Befriend them.

    And don't let them down.

3. **It's not who you know — it's who you trust.** Ultimately your success will be judged by what you deliver to yourself, your family, your friends, your investors, your stockholders — all those people who put their faith in you.

    You have to get to trust.

You have to reach out and find the experts needed.

You must connect with the backers, builders and bankers, your employers or mentors, as well as that guy or gal of your dreams.

You have to commit to those relationships.

You and you alone must get to trust with each of them.

You must assure that so long as you are connected, that trust will endure.

At the heart of every successful business, career, or life of joy is a man or woman of integrity.

One.

You.

The Shortest Distance

Tyler was completely confounded.

Over lunch he told me what had happened. He runs an animation company and had been trying for months to get in to see the folks at a major advertising agency that could definitely use his services.

"I've sat in their reception room so long, and so many times I know it better than their new receptionist does," he said.

He'd given up. And then, he tried again. This time it was with the agency's client. Another reception room, another new receptionist. He requested their company directory and was told that it was "all on computer."

Frustrated, he told his friend Mindy his woes. She volunteered that her cousin worked at the company and that she would be glad to put Tyler in contact with him.

Tyler was invited to look at the directory on the cousin's computer. He did not pass go or collect $200 or roll the dice — he went straight to the company at animated character speed. The cousin, after learning why Tyler wanted the directory, said, "Wouldn't you just rather meet the marketing and agency teams? They'll all be here in a few minutes."

Tyler was introduced; collected business cards and was granted access to both the agency and the client. By simply telling a friend what he was trying to do, he had, in one afternoon, accomplished what had been impossible for months.

He summarized the story over lunch and concluded, "I just don't get it. I only met these people by some kind of fluke accident."

Accident? Hardly. Sometimes the shortest distance between you and what you want is not the direct approach. It is the same whether you are pursuing a sale like Tyler, looking for your first job, or trying to link up with that "special someone." Hierarchical thinking in a web world leads only to confusion.

The links today are webs: the World Wide Web of the Internet, Intranets (the web inside corporations), and most importantly, the individual webs of influence we call personal networks.

Tyler was nearly stymied by a printed directory absorbed by the Intranet. He made contact through a personal network but didn't really understand how or why it worked.

To build a business, a career, or a life of joy, you need to recognize the best way to connect, and then adapt your approach.

Let's start with the Internet. Most companies that have some presence on the net will let you know by posting their addresses in all the places where you might find other contact information. Or, when asked, will proudly give you their URL or World Wide Web address. With that, you can *find out more than you might in multiple sales calls.*

Looking for a job? Never before has it been so easy to get information on established companies. You can learn what is important to them and be certain it is important to you.

Personal sites can be even more revealing. And lots of folks have them. Don't hesitate to ask a professional if he or she has a web site. It might open doors that you never knew existed.

People and companies tend to reveal more on their web pages than they do in conversation. The reason is that they are attempting to generate credibility. They try to do it through candor, which works in face-to-face conversation. But in this situation they aren't getting the feedback that causes them to stop short of revealing too much. Hence, you can learn a great deal about a company without ever leaving your computer.

An Intranet, or company network, is a different story. In most cases you'll have zero access to this corporately-controlled connection with its underlying data. Treat any invitation to let your curiosity romp here with the greatest diplomacy. It is better not to do so without a formal agreement in place.

Personal diplomacy, as former President Bush describes networking, can be just as productive. Tyler connected. You can, too. You *can* identify the nodes, the people that are linked. That, too, is easy.

Do you have one acquaintance in town who knows where to get everything, or has the right person to solve your problem, or knows exactly who to call to find out? That person is a local node. She or he is a connection point for many people, all seeking assistance.

There are regional and national and international nodes as
well. You can identify them by determining just how far away
the calls they get are coming from.

To succeed in today's fast-paced world, you need to find the
right partners and those nodes, if not the right one, can usually
help in your search.

On a personal level, seek out men and women who will help
you with no expectation of reward. These are people who, on
hearing that you need something, respond with the words,
"How can I help?"

For business, think about the products and services your
prospect needs. Seek out the companies that provide them and
ask for help. Develop ongoing relationships with the providers
of services that your clients and customers need, and refer
them. They will return the favor. Ask your clients or customers
if they have a vendor or supplier that does business with the
prospect. Contact them and ask for a hand.

Webs of influence have many points of contact. Those webs
will increase in the future. They will grow wider and wider.

Start building your contacts today and stay in touch with
them. Build ongoing relationships starting now. You'll need
them to help you decide when to go direct, when to select
another point of contact, and when to take the "great circle
route."

In today's world you often have to put your trust in somebody
else to get the message through. Choose well and it's well
worth it.

A Razor-Sharp Mind In a Rumpled Suit

My friend Bob is a Management Consultant — a real one.

He's not between jobs. It's what he does for a living.

He's known for his razor-sharp mind and his ability to get to the heart of a problem in a hurry. Bob does it with questions. Question after question, each answer inexorably leading to another question. Clients, former clients, and folks who have worked with him all agree that he is a business force to be reckoned with.

But Bob has a problem. He is one of those people who somehow, within seconds of dressing, becomes rumpled. I've seen this man extract a freshly laundered and starched shirt from the box, don it and inside of two minutes look like he slept in it. He is the only man I know who can put on a custom tailored $1000 suit and immediately look like he's been out in the rain on a construction site all day long.

Then there's his raincoat. It's a spendy London Fog type, beautifully constructed with the attention to detail you only find in European shops. Unfortunately, the coat always looks like it was thrown in the back of an open jeep used for the inspection of all 72 wells in an oilfield yesterday. And that's on a good day!

I ran into him one evening at a Chamber of Commerce meeting just as he was hanging the coat up. He started telling me about how his clients had come up with a new way to describe what he does. Then, mid-explanation, caught the eye of another visitor, said "I'll get back to you," and embarked on one of his questioning forays as they left me standing in the coatroom.

Multiple times that evening Bob and I crossed paths and each time a similar pattern ensued. He'd get to the point of that description and then get lured away.

It made me think, though, of what it takes to stand out in a crowd.

It is not easy. It never has been. Not even in Ancient Greece, according to Aesop.

In those days, when men were allowed to have many wives, a middle-aged man had one wife who was older, and one who was young. Each loved him very much, and desired to see him look more like herself.

Now the man's hair was turning gray, which the young wife didn't like as it made him look too old to be her husband. So each night she would comb his hair and pluck out the white ones.

But the older wife saw her husband growing gray with pleasure. So every morning, as she helped him dress for the day, she would arrange his hair and gently pull out as many of the black ones as she could.

The consequence was that the man soon found himself bald.

The moral of the story is: Please all and you will please none. Aesop understood that you cannot be all things to all people.

You must be singular.

The moxie of my friend Enid's business card that proclaims "Copywriter, rock star, human" in the title slot, and then at the bottom in italics says, "Okay, so I'm not a rock star, but I once had a Janis Joplin lunchbox" blows me away each time I read it.

Tom Peterson's, "and free is a very good price!" though predictable, is quintessentially Tom.

Each of them stands out from the crowd. Each is successful. Each, in her or his own way, is a leader, and somehow different from the masses.

Some call it charisma.

Others believe it's a form of brazenness. They call it chutzpah.

In business, your career and yes, life in general, it comes from congruity — taking a position and sticking to it.

It is that part of your personality that separates you from the pack.

I call it singularity.

Each of us has some, but like athletic skill and intelligence and all the other complex characteristics of being human, it's not evenly distributed. Yet each of us, undeniably, has a quality, strength, or viewpoint that endows us with a oneness. It is what makes a person unique, a company identifiable, and gives products or services an impetus to succeed.

Can you find your singularity, build on it, and add to your success?

You bet! There are three easy steps:

1. Become an expert. Devote at least one hour each day for a year to the subject or area of your choice. Read about it. Do it. Experiment in it. Take a course in it. Immerse yourself and follow the side paths that open to you. Mastery of nearly any subject can be yours—if you'll do the work.

Also set aside at least 30 minutes each day to consider completely disconnected subjects. How? Pick up a magazine at the bookstore—one you've never read before. Stop into a museum or library or other public information venue and browse. Surf the net on a subject chosen by opening the dictionary and selecting a word at random.

Integrate what you've seen and heard into your area of expertise. You'll find that you'll now be able to talk more comfortably with a larger array of people about the subjects that are of interest to them while more easily connecting your expertise to theirs. You'll listen a little more carefully as your connections broaden. That will add to your allure.

Charisma can be built through confidence in your self, your expertise, a true interest in others, and a real desire to communicate.

2. Risk being different. Some of us already are. Most of us are shorter, taller, faster, slower, thinner, fatter, balder, or hairier, or some other "er." Rejoice if you have one of those obvious "ers" and can use it to your benefit. People remember people with any of them.

Some of us aren't that lucky. We have to find a way to become memorable. For one salesman, I've been told, it was literally changing his hat — to a homburg which wasn't in style at the time. And would you recognize a couple of circles atop a head as mouse ears if Disney hadn't been promoting all these years? Me, well, I grew a Vandyke beard and moustache more than thirty years ago, and have worn it ever since.

Changes in dress and appearance are only part of the equation, though. People need more than a visual reference. We judge, and are judged, on looks, words, and deeds.

Your words, as an expert, must make it easy for people to understand and connect your expertise to their experiences. Don't fall into the jargon trap. If someone can't understand what is done by you or your company, the fault is yours, not theirs.

You will be remembered for showing understanding, but referred on the basis of what you do. Actions still speak louder than words. The guys in Schwab tire stores run to get to your car. Nordstrom clerks send thank you cards. Quality Lead Management's telephone staffers call back exactly when they agreed to — to the minute.

As my British friends would say, "Be a little cheeky." People remember audacity. They forget timidity. Build a little chutz-pah into your approach to life.

3. Stick to it. It takes time for people to see the "new you." It takes time to convince people that you or your company are really experts.

My friend Bob is living proof. It takes people a while to see the razor-sharp mind inside the rumpled suit. As we were leaving that night, he still hadn't finished his story, but he turned as he was headed out the door and, pulling on that reprehensible-looking raincoat, asked, "Did I tell you what they're calling me is 'the Columbo of management consultants'?" Then he winked, turned and waving a hand, went out the door.

The character of a TV homicide detective played by Peter Falk matched Bob's image — the quiet brilliance, the incessant questions, even the ratty raincoat. His clients had found a way to refer him citing both the characteristics that set him apart. Bob found singularity by being himself and being a great deal like a character in a high-rated TV show.

It can happen to you, too.

Develop charisma, add a little chutzpah and stick to it. That's the way to singularity.

It takes time. But it is definitely worth it.

Pearl Diving: Building
A Gem Of a Personal Network

Pearl Diving?

Yes, pearl diving. Each time you dive into a meeting, float along in line at the supermarket or find yourself swept into a gathering of two or more people you can go pearl diving.

Plunge in. Start a conversation. Introduce yourself.

Network. You'll never know what you're going to find until you dive in.

Network. Learn about that person.

Network. Just don't try to turn that contact into a contract on the spot. It won't work.

We've all met people who try that. They glide up to you like a shark, ask a question, talk through your response with a rapid fire commercial, tell you to call them, and then they're gone.

In their view, they are networking. Those predatory types just don't understand the difference between transactional and relational networking.

Transactional networkers want to score now. They are driven to pin down a prospect, get the job, or close the deal. They have no time for anything else. They see networking as just one more form of manipulation. Leads groups that penalize members for failure to produce prospects fall into this category, as do the tactics employed by some multi-level marketing organizations.

There is a place for transactions, but it is never on a first meeting. And in most cases it will come much later in the sequence.

The best networkers understand that networking is the establishment of a relationship.

Relational networkers aren't interested in what you might be worth to them. They are always more curious about you as a person. They consistently ask how they can be of help to you rather than the other way around. They maintain the contact out of regard for you, not a need to cash in on the contact.

Relational networkers are pearl divers. They understand that each of us is like a pearl.

Like a pearl, we've added layer upon layer of experience.

Like a pearl, we've rolled around and around in the narrow confines of our lives.

Like a pearl, we hide most of ourselves beneath a glossy surface.

No two of us are the same. Yet we respond similarly to someone who expresses a genuine interest in us.

Each of us has qualities that make us jewels. The gentle wash of friendship makes us glow. We return a little care, a little concern with sharing. We share our experience, our knowledge, our trusted resources, with someone who has taken the time to care about us.

"But I'm shy," you say. I can't just start talking to a stranger.

I'm shy, too. But I learned that just dipping your toes in the water doesn't work. You've got to dive in. Early on I played a game with myself at company events and cocktail parties and in crowded theater and checkout lines to get started. I tried to identify the people as creatures of the sea.

The shark you already know about. Others I found were:

> *The Hermit Crab*. At a party, this denizen of the deep can be found in a corner near the food. Or looking out at the view. Or quietly seated as if waiting for the next event. The hermit crab is always alone. Direct eye contact is avoided.

But all it takes is for you to say, "Hello, what brings you here?" to get them out of their shells. Once, my friend Jan approached a young man staring raptly out the windows of the room in a business tower where she was to address an association luncheon meeting. He told her that he was new in town and was attending hoping to find advisers to help him invest the half-million dollars the sale of his business in another city had netted him.

After the meeting, she asked if he had met anyone. He answered, "No, you were the only one who introduced herself to me." The following week she introduced him to three entrepreneurs over lunch.

If she had not decided to say hello to the hermit crab, would he ever have gotten out of his shell?

> *The Octopus.* Easily recognized by the person
> trapped in its physical and verbal grasp. The guy or
> gal looking totally uncomfortable is the victim and
> someone who will be grateful to you for a rescue.

Richard, an ad exec friend, told me about an Octopus he ran across in the line at an airport car rental counter. The obtuse vacationer was holding his elbow in a vise-like grip and jawing away at him to his obvious dismay.

A well-tailored business woman behind them simply asked, "Are you here on a business trip, too?" She was greeted by Richard's beaming face and a whispered, "Thank you."

They exchanged business cards and the following week met in her hometown. She did what you should do on finding Octopi. Rescue the damsel or guy in distress. That is always profitable whether you advance your career, make a sale or wind up, like Richard, with a new light in your life.

There is an ocean of possibilities that exist to build your business, your career, and a life of joy. Trust in those pearls of relationships, those gems of contacts that will do for you the one thing that only networking can do so effectively – put people who know and care about you to work making new contacts for you.

Build those relationships. Depend on individuals, not corporations. Put your faith in people, not contracts. You can be confident they will send you business, refer you, and delight in your happiness.

Careers and companies and lives of joy are built one contact at
a time. Develop one pearl of a relationship plus another and
yet another until you have a multi-strand string—each a
unique and memorable personality adding to all the others.

That is the pearl hidden at the heart of networking. Each of
you is an asset for the other. Each enhances the value of all.

Dive in. The water's fine.

Ladder of Dreams

I've done some crazy things to make sure people get the point.

Early on, I started a speech by coming on stage, climbing to the top of a step ladder, taking a seat, and beginning with these words:

> "Every entrepreneur has a dream. Something you strive for. The place you want to get to.
>
> "For some of us it's no more than a schematic imagined in a catnap. But for most it's a full-color castle way up there in the air.
>
> "How are you going to get there?
>
> "How can you get to your castle in the air?
>
> "You have to find the ladder."

Today, more than ever, you need to find that ladder.

You find it by understanding how to generate referrals from people who can help you — step by step — climb the ramparts to your castle in the air.

Most of us believe it is just good sense to get input before we make decisions on simple things.

Before you go to a movie you'll usually check with a friend to get his or her opinion. When you're looking for a new restaurant it's only natural to ask folks where you work for suggestions. We continually ask for advice from friends and acquaintances on all sorts of topics: restaurants, movies, cars, where to sit at a concert, dates, campsites, vacations, diets, you name it.

For those small decisions we lust after guidance from family, friends, acquaintances, virtually anyone who, we believe, has a scintilla more information or experience than we do.

And we call it common sense.

Yet, though we use our common sense in these simple matters, we tend to lose sight of human nature when the stakes get higher. Somehow, when we're the one others must consider, we forget that a referral carries more weight than a well-known name.

As we open the doors of our businesses, we simply hope that customers will come. We ask others to "do the marketing." Looking for a job we start perusing those completely impersonal want ads. Building a career, we decide to rely only on hard work. Searching for that special person, we loiter in public places trying to build up the courage to say hello.

And it doesn't work.

It takes gathered wisdom to realize that the customers you are seeking, the job that will advance your career, and that person you want to impress, can best be reached through referrals.

It takes that shared wisdom to realize that it takes a ladder to
get to your castle way up there in the air—a ladder of dreams.
Each step up is slightly more complex. Each gets you closer to
your goal. Each reduces the amount you have to sell. Each
brings you closer to your dream.

Getting started is easy. Tell your family, friends and acquaintances the kind of person you're looking for. This works regardless of whether you call that person a customer or client, a
new boss or a mentor, a friend or a fiancee. Now talk to the
folks they suggest, and the ones they suggest, and so on.

Remember that it is human nature to want help with decisions.
It is natural and normal for people to respond positively and
pass you on to those they believe might be of help to you.

Most times people are looking for multiple resources. How
you are referred to them makes all the difference.

Here, in ascending order, are the steps up the referral ladder:

Fifth Step:	Endorsement
Fourth Step:	Testimonial
Third Step:	Recommendation
Second Step:	Introduction
First Step:	Pointer

Here's how to identify each step and climb to the next:

The Pointer merely suggests other people you might talk to. This referral literally points to others and takes no proactive action to help you.

To get the most out of a pointer, ask:

1. Which of these would be best for my need?
2. May I use your name?

That at least gets you to the next level.

The Impersonal Introduction leads to you making a telephone call or otherwise contacting someone and saying, "(Referral's name) said I should call you..." That, many times, is good enough to get you through the first line of defense whether it is a gatekeeper or the armor of a person of power.

But that is all it buys you. You are on your own to convince that person of your capabilities. You are the one who must be proactive. You do the calling. You do the follow-up. You must generate the enthusiasm, believability and interest.

In both the first and second steps you must act. The person making the referral is in contact with you only. Getting her or him to agree to additional actions in your behalf will get you up to the next step. Here's how to make that happen:

1. Could I have (person's name) call you for your reactions to my qualifications?

2. Would you be willing to pass along a copy of my bro-
    chure, resume, data, that tells about me or my service?

That can move you one step higher in the hierarchy.

The Personal Recommendation is the first time that your
referrer is actively assisting you. A note or a letter that accom-
panies a copy of your materials that simply says, "(Person's
Name,) take a look at this" is sufficient to get you reviewed in
some cases.

The best way to assure this situation is to suggest:

> "If you'll just jot a note now on your stationery, I'll
> attach a copy, pay the postage and assure that it gets
> in the mail today."

But how do you go a step higher?

It's not easy from here on. They are literally lending you their
credibility. It's best if you let them volunteer.

But if you feel you need to climb one rung further you need
to ask:

1. Could you call (person's name) now to encourage her/
    him to see me? It would probably be much easier for
    you to get through than me.
2. Would you ask what day I might buy him/her lunch?

That is a big step.

The Telephone Testimonial occurs when the person you're talking to picks up the phone and provides a testimonial for you as you listen.

There is only one step better than that.

You won't get there without asking or having a track record with the referrer. Usually both will be required.

You must be the kind of person who gets results.

The top step is:

The Personal Endorsement which occurs when the referrer agrees to endorse you personally in an introductory meeting with the prospect. The referrer sets up the meeting, convinces the prospect to attend, and relies on their friendship or mutual respect to assure attendance.

The referrer becomes your coach, confidante and cohort.

From here, you're above the mass of people looking for a way to build their businesses or careers or find that special person. You're operating on a whole different level.

Careful, it can get heady up there in your castle way up in the air. Don't forget what got you there.

The Ward Boss Software Solution

I don't know where I heard this story or whether or not it's true, but it is one of the ways I came to understand this business of networking, so here goes...

Back in the days of big city ward politics there was a ward boss in Chicago or New York or wherever, who was considered the best, both by his constituents and by the city, state, and federal politicians who needed his help to get into office.

He had a reputation for having a fantastic memory, and knowing everything about the people in his ward as well as the politicians who came to him for help.

One day one of those politicos asked Farley how he did it. He pulled that two-inch stub of a dead cigar from his mouth and said, " I keep files."

The young politician, who had learned that listening is at the heart of great conversation and gathering wisdom, simply said, "Oh," and waited.

In a moment, Farley went on, "And I have an office with an anteroom, as I'm sure you noticed. Whenever someone comes in, my secretary gets their name and asks them to wait just a moment. Then she steps in here to see if I'm ready to visit with them, goes over to those file cabinets, pulls the file, and gives it to me along with any observations she's made in the ante-room. I take two or three minutes to review the file and then signal her to send them in.

"Because of the file, I know their names, the names of their kids, if any, and a wealth of other information about them. That information has been gathered over time, and because I'm sincerely interested in them, following our meeting I note anything new I've found out in the file.

"Take that couple who were in here before you, for instance. He's lost his job at the warehouse and she's worried that the savings are going to run out before he finds another job. What they didn't say that the file tells me is that their son, who is studying violin, might have to stop and go to work. That would be shame. You should hear that kid play!

"Anyway, they're good kids and they just need a break. I sent him to see a businessman who owes me a favor. He'll get a job and I'll get a vote. More importantly, their kid will bring joy into a lot of hearts."

Then, back to his gruff self, Farley growled, "So I made a note in their file about what happened and the fact that she's ex-pecting in five months, and there's a note here for my secretary to call her mother the month the baby is due so we can know when to send a card."

He went on, "The real trick though is that I have a card file that helps me keep track of other things. I sort people by name, geography, and profession. That way, if I need to find out about something in another part of town or another town, I just look them up. That's where I start. The complete

files aren't kept on everybody, just the ones who are important to me."

The Farley File.
You need one, too, because businesses, careers, and lives of joy
are built one connection at a time. One connection plus another, yet another, and still another until you have a crowd.

Simply making contact is not enough.

You have to have a systematic way to assure that you make
those contacts, store information about them, quickly refer
them to one another, build relationships, maintain them, and
make them mutually profitable.

But none of us remembers everything. The less frequently
we are involved with any individual, the less we remember
about them. Unfortunately, that's the way our wetware
works. We're human. We forget. We need memory aids. It
takes us time to build relationships. And sometimes we
don't maintain them so well.

In this case, hardware and software are better suited to the
task.

Most people believe that having a Personal Digital Assistant
(PDA) is the answer. Those palm top devices are wonderful for
carrying addresses and calendars, but they don't have all the
capabilities you need to emulate Farley.

Even if you use a PDA, get professional-level contact management software for your major computer whether it is home,
desktop, or laptop. That will allow you to keep all the information you need and do it with ease.

Don't be fooled by software that looks like an address book on the screen or has you schedule meetings or to-dos that are not attached to the record of the person who is involved with that task or meeting. Your software needs to link actions, comments, observations, e-mails, letters and memos, and even phone calls to the record of that individual. How else will you have a record of what has caused your relationship to develop?

Million Dollar Advice. Most importantly, take this simple step to be sure that a relationship does develop. Upon completion of any action with an individual, at the first opportunity, schedule your next action with that individual. Then, when the computer reminds you to take action, follow your own direction.

That advice has doubled the business of more than one company. It made me a million dollars one morning. It got the job for more candidates than I can count. It helps young couples really find one another.

And Farley assures me it kept him in office for many years.

Gary and the Restaurant Guide

Last week Gary's phone rang.

It was Jean. She's the executive secretary for the president of a very large commercial contractor located a plane trip away from his home.

Gary had taken the time to get acquainted with her while he was phoning for a meeting with her boss. When he got into town he renewed the acquaintance and asked her if she could suggest a place for dinner. Jean told him about a quiet little restaurant overlooking the lake, that she liked to go to for special occasions.

Gary and his wife, who had joined him on the trip, thoroughly enjoyed the meal. They enjoyed it so much that when he wrote a personal note to say thanks the next day he enclosed a gift certificate for two for her.

It wasn't that much when you consider the fact that his meeting had netted a six-figure contract. He's just that kind of guy. When someone does him a favor, he says "thank you" and goes on about his business. Gary is a gem of a networker. He doesn't expect a reward for his every act.

That's what made Jean's call so important. She didn't have to call. But she did.

She didn't have to save his card. But she did.

She didn't have to pass his name on to the executive secretaries in their San Francisco and Denver operations. But she did.

She didn't have to fax his credentials to their office in Phoenix for the contract he just landed. But she did.

Why did she call?

She called to tell him she had been back to that little restaurant twice. Once to take a special guy to dinner. The second time was with the same fellow. Only this time it was a really special dinner. Her engagement ring came with dessert.

Why did Jean call? She just wanted to say thank you.

I heard about all this when Gary called me for the name of a friend in the art business. It seems that Jean had mentioned a sculptor back when they had first met and he had noted the fact and since there's a wedding coming up and he's invited — well, you get the picture.

Who is this guy? At the time he met Jean he was the principal of a three-person consulting firm which he had founded. Although Gary is not an engineer (not even a college graduate), AT&T concluded that he was the only one for the job.

How did that happen? More importantly, how can you make it happen for you?

Be a crowd of one
Building a business, a career, or finding the love of your life are all about your ability to connect with people. Professionals

get that designation by having a talent, developing it, and
practicing their skills until they can deliver predictable results.

Know your limits, your resources, and how to commit to
relationships. You, and you alone, must get to trust with all of
them. At the heart of every successful business, career, or life
of joy is a man or woman of integrity.

Take the Shortest Distance
Sometimes the shortest distance between you and your objective is a circle rather than a straight line. Networking is your
ticket to "the great circle route." Trust is what makes it fly.

Rely on the connections you have made and don't expect the
direct route to be the most efficient. That job you're seeking in
Phoenix might happen because of an interview in Denver.
That casual acquaintance at the newsstand might lead to the
venture capital you need. A family member could introduce
you to the guy or gal of your dreams.

Make yourself singular
To be remembered, you need to stand out from the crowd.
Take the time to become an expert. You can do this in one hour
a day for a year! Charisma can be built through confidence in
your self, your expertise, a true interest in others, and a real
desire to communicate.

Then risk being different. Actions still speak louder than
words. As my British friends would say, "Be a little cheeky."
People remember audacity. They forget timidity. Build a little
Chutzpah into your approach to life.

And stick to it. It takes time for people to see the "new you." It
takes time. But congruity is definitely worth it.

Go Pearl Diving
Plunge in. Start a conversation. Introduce yourself. Network. Listen. Show genuine interest. Enjoy the moment without expectation of additional reward.

Careers and companies and lives of joy are all built one contact at a time. Develop one pearl of a relationship plus another and yet another until you have a multi-strand string—each a unique and memorable personality adding to all the others.

Find your Ladder
You find it by understanding how to generate referrals from people who can help you—step by step—climb the ramparts to your castle in the air. The customers you are seeking, the job that will advance your career, and that guy or gal you want to impress, can best be reached through referrals. But you have to ask.

Build your Farley File
It's all about contacts. You have to have a systematic way to assure that you make them, store information about them, quickly refer them to one another, build relationships, maintain them, and make them mutually profitable.

The wetware, that computer we carry around on our shoulders, isn't up to the task. Hardware and software are better suited.

Regardless of what system you use, you can guarantee positive results if you decide your next action with the individual on completing the current action, note the "to do" and the date. And when the date comes up, take the action planned.

Amass Your String of Pearls
Do it with integrity. Count on trust. Be "a little cheeky."
Plunge in and build relationships with no reward in mind. Ask
for referrals and find a systematic way to keep track of all
those gems of contacts.

Joining
Your Flame
With Others

The Insights

What have we learned about wisdom?

Cheryl summed it up for us:

As you move forward in your chosen career, whatever it is, be sure to seek out wise counsel to help you get off onto the right foot, and to remain on solid footing. Many people have tried to go it alone. For some, it has worked. But for the majority of others, wise counsel would have saved them much heartache, thousands and thousands of dollars, and irretrievable hours of wasted time.

The authors of this book, the members of Speakers Quorum, have been meeting for years and enjoy a wonderful camaraderie, sharing of ideas, and professional support. Where one person lacks knowledge, another has that information. As a result, we have our built-in team of advisors when it comes to various aspects of the speaking, consulting, and training business. We've grown to care for each other and are willing to listen, and freely offer a different perspective. It helps us build confidence, refine our products and services, and provides a sounding board for new ideas. We are all in similar businesses (speaking and consulting) but our specialties are in different areas, eliminating any person feeling the need to be competitive with any other in our group.

On the other hand, we need other advisors as well. These other advisors are those outside the realm of speaking, consulting, and training, and include those such as attorneys, accountants, bankers, investment personnel, and a variety of other "team counsel" members. To operate our businesses effectively, we must be aware of certain laws and regulations, how to be good stewards of our finances, etc. We recognize the wisdom in seeking out the counsel of those who know about these matters.

Al enhanced that need for others and how to approach them in his parting comments:

My view of wisdom is that it is reflected best in short, insightful statements about one's self and others. Here are eight insights that I find especially valuable:

- Wisdom, resiliency, professionalism, and other high-level human attributes can be learned, but they can't be taught.

- It is in our human nature to judge others by their actions, ourselves by our explanations. We attribute bad motives to others, but have good reasons for doing what we do.

- When someone tells me how horribly they've been treated, it is smart to go hear the other party's explanations.

- Most people with positive attitudes have negative attitudes about negative attitudes. When I turn negativity experts into valuable resources, things work much better.

- Thinking that things would be better if only others would change is true, but it won't happen. The best way to get others to change how they act toward me, is for me to change how I act toward them.

- After a distressing experience, when I replace "If only..." thinking with "Next time..." thinking, I learn good lessons and look forward to the future with confidence and optimism.

- The best way to handle conflict is to listen actively so that the other party feels well heard.

- When I'm in a difficult situation, the best way to get a good outcome is to ask myself "How can I interact with this so that things work out well for all of us?"

Gail had much the same take, expressing her view of the journey to wisdom in this way:

Look for the good stuff in any bad stuff. You'll feel better. And when you feel better, you can do better. And better becomes a habit.

Now, the bad stuff is going to come your way, no matter how positive you are. That's part of life.

No one, including you and me, is entitled to constant happiness—not in this life. As a matter of dismal fact, you and I are not "entitled" to much of anything. It's up to us to earn what we get. And sometimes we don't get it, even when we have earned it. That's part of life, too. So accept the bad when it comes, but don't expect it. You have better things to do with your time.

One of them is planning. When you have your act together, it's remarkable how productive you can be. So play a game of "what if" with yourself. "What if" this happens; "what if" that happens. Develop a quick plan for what you will, or will not, do, under a variety of circumstances. That way you will be able to deal with whatever comes your way, and get on with it.

Look for the positives in your daily contacts — co-workers, customers, clients. Think, and speak about them in positive terms. It will unblock energy you didn't know you had! Look for the positives in every situation — acknowledge your mistakes, but concentrate on what you did right!

Value time. Maintain a daily planner that shows you when you need to be where, and will reflect how you have invested your day. Honor your commitments. Be where you say you will be, when you say you will be, prepared with what you said you would have. If you can't, let the person who is counting on you know as soon as possible.

If you are employed, anticipate what needs to happen for the good of your company or organization. Maintain your values.

Treasure your friends and watch your enemies, but don't be paranoid about them. The best way to deal with your enemies is to make them your friends — but only if that's a reasonable approach. You are no one's door mat.

Always take calls from family. Decide who, or what comes first. If it's your work, don't get married. If you're married, don't have children. If you have children, it's time to change your priorities.

Jerry, the Networking Ninja, concurred with his colleagues, saying:

You are not alone.

You are part of something more.

Always.

You are connected.

Choose to react positively.

Elect to help without reward.

Listen. Care. Say so.

And fortune will smile on you.

Even as you seek others' wisdom,

Prepare.

Your advice will be sought

Perhaps when you least expect it.

The Authors

Cheryl Matschek, M.S., M.H.

Cheryl Matschek is President of The Cheryl Matschek Company, Inc., Soaring Horizons®, and Princess Publishing, based in Portland, Oregon. She is an internationally known professional speaker, trainer, consultant, and author.

Cheryl holds a Bachelor's degree in psychology, a Master's degree in behavioral science, a Master's in herbology and is currently completing her Ph.D. in Natural Health, Nutrition and Iridology, and she is a Certified Iridologist. Cheryl has appeared on television and radio talk shows, is the author of several books and articles, and has produced numerous audio cassettes.

Cheryl's vast knowledge, experience, and tremendous insight in business has helped businesses and organizations to become more successful in the areas of leadership, team development, sales and marketing, personal potential, and health. Today she specializes in the areas of leadership, health, and professional practice development, speaking at conferences, conventions, business meetings, and retreats. She is a dynamic individual with challenging messages that have helped change the lives of thousands. Cheryl brings a tremendous wealth of knowledge to business, offering valuable insights and how-to's for developing business and professional teams that are productive, committed, and fun, and building profitable, successful businesses and professional practices that generate satisfaction and fulfillment for all involved.

Prior to beginning her professional speaking career in 1979, Cheryl was a highly successful life insurance agent and Million Dollar Round Table producer for the New York Life Insurance Company, and went on to become one of five women in sales management in the United States, Puerto Rico and Canada for the same company at age 28.

In addition to her speaking career, in the mid-90's Cheryl developed a natural health practice which she continues today. Although the demands of her speaking career and natural health practice are many, Cheryl pays attention to balance in her life. She and her husband, J. Norman Matschek, D.M.D., a cosmetic and family dentist in the Portland, Oregon area enjoy their time together growing spiritually and actively participating in their church, traveling, reading, golfing, and relaxing, to remain spiritually, mentally, and physically fit. Learn more about Cheryl at:

www.Matschek.com or
www.soaringhorizons.com

Jerry Fletcher, The Networking Ninja

Jerry Fletcher is President of Z-axis Marketing, Inc., the Founder of NeXtworking.com, author of two books and five audio programs.

This former CEO is an expert at business development who has raised over $500,000 in private funding for a client in just 17 days, increased the first quarter sales of a consulting firm by over $1.2 Million with a single suggestion, and introduced over 200 new products and services — successfully.

Jerry's strategic marketing consultancy focuses on customer-oriented product development and referral-based sales and marketing. His carefully-crafted techniques and technologies are guaranteed to put your untapped potential to work to build businesses, careers, and lives of joy.

He *is* the "Networking Ninja," a professional speaker known for his "Endnotes" (closing keynotes) that give audiences both the motivation and the methods to get to the next level. The Ninja "sends 'em home smokin' and brings 'em back next year beggin' for more." Learn more at:

www. NetworkingNinja.com.

Al Siebert, Ph.D.

Dr. Al Siebert is Director of The Resiliency Center. He is internationally recognized for his research into the inner nature of highly resilient survivors. His book *The Survivor Personality* is now in its eleventh printing, and has been published in six languages. His popular quiz "How Resilient Are You?" has been featured in many publications. He has been interviewed on *National Public Radio*, the *NBC Today Show*, and *OPRAH*.

He is an ex-paratrooper with a Ph.D. in psychology from the University of Michigan. He taught management psychology at Portland State University for over thirty years. He served as chairman of his county school board, and was a volunteer rap group leader with Vietnam veterans.

Al Siebert speaks frequently at conferences for government agencies, health care, Native American, and professional groups.

More information about his resiliency talks and materials can be found at the Resiliency Center web site:

www.ResiliencyCenter.com.

Gail Tycer, M.S.

Gail Tycer is a professional writer and editor, columnist, speaker, consultant, and coach. She has spent a lifetime studying and teaching the thought process that results in clear, fast, results-oriented writing: what it takes to make a message concise, compelling, convincing. She shares the fascinating results of this continuing study through her workshops, presentations, and consulting nationwide.

Gail has been an advertising agency president, public relations director, radio and television personality and executive, and college professor. As marketing strategist and professional speaker, Gail has worked with top national and international firms. She is the author of the the Quick-Study Guides to strategic business communication, and has published materials ranging from books and articles for the popular market to highly technical material for specialized audiences.

Gail is a professional member of the National Speakers Association. She has earned both graduate and undergraduate degrees in communication, focusing on business applications of communication theory, methods, and techniques. Gail was a founding director of the Oregon Writers

Colony, and was among the first recipients nationwide of the Certified Business Communicator designation. She was elected delegate to the White House Conference on Small Business in Washington, D.C.

Selected strategic business communication articles, and additional information about Gail's workshops, talks, and materials can be found at:

www.GailTycer.com

Index

 **may be ordered individually or in quantity for groups, employee or member gifts, or awards—any time you feel that the counsel gathered between these covers will be of help to individuals or organizations.**

Order Form (copy this page)

	Quantity	Price	Total
Please send me	_____copies at	$20.00 each	$_____
	Handling & Shipping	$2.00 each	$_____
		Total Order	$_____

Ordering more than 10 copies

Please send me	_____copies at	$15.00 each	$_____
	Handling & Shipping	$1.00 each	$_____
		Total Order	$_____

Name (please print) _____

Address_____

City_____ State _____ Zip _____

Phone_____

Return a copy of this order form with check or money order payable to:
Practical Psychology Press
PO Box 535
Portland, OR 97207
503/289-3295

If paying with credit card, please complete the items below:
  Visa   Mastercard   Number_____

Expires _____ Signature _____

Meet the authors in person!

These four entertaining and informative professional speakers regularly bring their upbeat and inspiring messages to corporations and organizatons across North America.

The pragmatic advice and the zest for living portrayed in these pages is available for your regional and national conferences, conventions, and meetings throughout the year.

For a keynote that opens your gathering in style, a content-laden breakout session, or an endnote that sends them home fired up, contact the authors at the Quorum web site.

Brilliant openers,
illuminating in-betweeners,
and sparkling closers

www.SpeakersQuorum.com

Speaker's Quorum

A shining array of speakers from the Pacific Northwest

If you have a personal story of how our book was useful to you, or a wisdom insight you'd like to share, please send it to us at our website:

GatheringWisdom.com